76 Minutes

My Search for Andrew, Alexander and Tanner Skelton

Ordering Information

Additional copies of *76 Minutes: My Search for Andrew, Alexander and Tanner Skelton* may be purchased for $17.95, plus $4 shipping and handling, from Faded Banner Publications, P.O. Box 101, Bryan, OH 43506, telephone 1-888-799-3787 (toll free), or on the Web at www.fadedbanner.com. Dealer inquiries are welcome.

76 Minutes

My Search for Andrew, Alexander and Tanner Skelton

By Lynn Thompson

Faded Banner Publications
Bryan, Ohio

Library of Congress Control Number: 2018966621

76 Minutes: My Search for Andrew, Alexander and Tanner Skelton

By Lynn Thompson

Edited By Don Allison

Cover design by Stuart Rosebrock

ISBN 978-0-9659201-9-3

First Printing

*For those who searched
and still remember*

Acknowledgments

Anything of value in this book started with Bill Rivera, who is not mentioned in it, so I would like to thank him up front.

As a retired lieutenant colonel, Bill had a contract to train young staff officers like me but he was never just a contractor. Every Soldier was Bill's Soldier and any staff puke who didn't do right by them didn't deserve to be in Bill's Army. He was big on understanding doctrine but not using it because "How the hell can you think outside the box if you don't know which one you're in?"

He was all about using the "Science of Control" to win the fight before anyone ever fired a shot and his analytical approach was the heartbeat of my narrative. I just flipped it over and ran it backwards. He never said we had to climb out of the box head first.

My other great mentor has been Don Allison, senior editor of The Bryan Times. Storytelling is an art anyone can learn but it takes a lot of practice and Don was all about practice. For ten years, he tolerated my experiments in creativity while giving me time to fix my own mistakes and learn from them. We were always on deadline and he could have been a dictator, but he focused on developing writers to do the job right rather than just getting the job done.

Don's wife, Diane, also worked at The Times before they retired and working with them together was the best part of any day. I could never get them to disagree on anything but it was always fun to try.

I was supposed to settle down after the war but working at a newspaper is no place to do that. The best stories don't happen on schedule or anywhere near the office and my wife, Lori, has let me chase them all. I don't get to take the kids to fires anymore (our last father-son work night involved a meth lab explosion at a crack house) but she still encourages them to read the paper and ask questions. That makes my job worth more than the paycheck, even when they find my typos ... which they do a lot more than I'd like to admit.

Greg Hembree and Josiah Harness are brothers from my military family. They didn't know anything about the Skelton boys' disappearance until I asked for help with figuring it out. All they wanted to know was when and where they needed to be without asking why.

John Walsh was equally dedicated. Time is money on a sound stage but when I showed up for an interview on the set of "Abduction in the Heartland" he stopped everything for 45 minutes just so we could talk. That conversation cost him a lot more than I made with the next day's headline, but he couldn't have cared less.

Guys like Larry Weeks, Steve Towns, James Snively and Al Word had nothing to gain and their reputations to lose by talking to me, but they never hesitated. They were open and straightforward about what happened, even when I asked the unpleasant questions. That was no easy task after Black Lives Matter declared war on Blue.

Finally, I'd like to thank Tanya Zuvers. She was drug through the mud during the worst week of anyone's life and had no reason to treat any reporter fairly, but she always has. I hope this book helps bring her sons home.

Table of Contents

List of Illustrations

Preface

I was in bed and asleep when my editor called at 11:35 p.m. on Jan. 30, 2011. She said there was a shootout on Portland Street and she could hear the gunshots over the scanner and I needed to put on my "big boy pants" and get over there with a camera.

I drove slow.

Bryan Police Chief Jeff Arnold was running yellow crime scene tape across the street when I got there. He said it started with a drive-by at the station when a suspect in a white pickup truck fired two shots through the front door and a third into an empty cruiser.

He said they found his truck parked with the flashers on at the corner of Portland and Parkview a few minutes later. The driver was hiding behind the house across the street at 343 S. Portland. He opened fire with an AR-15 when they tried to check it out.

A third officer ran silent a block east of the scene. He crept up through the alley and across the back yard, then shot the suspect in the head from 20 feet away. The guy who lived at 343 S. Portland was 93 years old and he slept through the whole thing. He didn't wake up until his son called to make sure he was all right. The guy walked out onto the porch in his bathrobe just after midnight and he wasn't at all happy about the bullet holes in his siding. "By God somebody better pay for that," he said.

The shooter was Rudy Relue and his daughter Andrea Andrews had died in the old guy's driveway eight months before the attack.

Rudy Relue

It was a Friday night on May 29, 2010, and Andrews had just met Adam Weisner at O'Bryan's Pub and Sports Bar. She was there for a graduation party. Her designated driver had one too many but so did Weisner. He threw back a few beers at a buddy's house and slammed a few more while he was talking to Andrews before he offered her a ride home on his motorcycle.

Seconds later he rolled through a stop sign, right in front of a cop. When the lights and sirens came on Weisner took off like a bat out of hell and crashed trying to make the turn on to Portland Street. Andrews flew off the back of his bike, hit the old guy's house and died at the scene.

Weisner, 23, got six years for aggravated vehicular homicide and went public with his story after rehab. "I hope you do not pity me," he said. "I deserve to be here."

Relue never saw it that way. He blamed police for what happened. He survived the shooting with a traumatic brain injury. He's still serving a seven-year sentence for felonious assault at the state prison in Lancaster.

Those three police officers are still in Bryan and probably will be when Relue gets out. Their kids still go to school here and still play ball in Garver Park on the weekends. They still trust their friends and their neighbors and the guys in their Monday night Bible studies. They still trust that things tend to work out if you do the right things the right way for the right reasons but that's hard when you know that they don't. Somebody died because they tried to keep them from getting killed and somebody tried to kill them because of it.

Steve Towns is the same way.

We grew up in West Unity. He graduated from Hilltop High School a year ahead of me but it could have been two. I was an August baby, the youngest and smallest in my class. I got homesick and cried within my first hour of kindergarten and then my pants fell down at recess and I cried some more. Hilltop was a really small school, less than 50 students per class, so I was a marked man until I graduated.

I don't think I ever talked to Towns when we were kids because I can't remember what he looked like. That's kind of a compliment. I used to keep a list of everyone I hated in school and just about everybody was on it.

Towns always wanted to be cop. He got his first job at the county jail in 1989 and got elected Williams sheriff in 2012. I never knew what I wanted to be. I went to college and majored in English literature because the department head promised "You can talk your way onto any job you want!" I ended up stocking shelves at Kmart until I joined the Army. I enlisted as a medic just because that's what Ernest Hemingway did and I haven't read any of his books since. I did talk my way into Officer Candidate School though and branched Infantry about a month before the 911 attacks. I spent seven years as a "Guard bum" bouncing between Iraq deployments and special duty assignments until we started having kids and my wife insisted I get "a real job" in 2009.

I lined up a white-collar office job with an insurance company in Fort Wayne, Indiana, and started buying ugly ties but I've never worn them. A week before the insurance thing started a friend asked me to stop by his office, which happened to be The Bryan Times, and I've been a crime reporter ever since.

If Towns carries a hate list I should be somewhere near the bottom, between drunks who fight but don't drive and punks who break stuff for no reason. When a couple of them trashed his wife's parent's yard I took a picture and splashed it on the front page with the headline "Vandals mangle mother-in-law's mailbox."

Cops and reporters don't always get along but Towns is all right.

Andrew, Alexander and Tanner Skelton disappeared on Nov. 26, 2010, and I've been following the story ever since.

On Sept. 10, 2013, I walked into Towns' office and started asking questions. He barked like he always does but then he stopped. "Look," he said. "You know everything we know. There are a couple little details we're never going to tell you and that's just the way it's going to be. We're protecting the integrity of the investigation.

"They're little things," he said. "They're not game changers. You know everything else."

Nothing has changed since then. The kids are still out there, still missing, because the one guy who knows what happened won't talk.

That's why I wrote this book. This is what I know, and what I've learned since.

MISSING

Alexander Skelton   **Tanner Skelton**   **Andrew Skelton**

DOB: Nov 4, 2003	**DOB:** Oct 20, 2005	**DOB:** Nov 20, 2001
Age Now: 7	**Age Now:** 5	**Age Now:** 9
Sex: Male	**Sex:** Male	**Sex:** Male
Race: White	**Race:** White	**Race:** White
Hair: Brown	**Hair:** Blonde	**Hair:** Brown
Eyes: Brown	**Eyes:** Blue	**Eyes:** Brown
Height: 3'9" (114 cm)	**Height:** 3'6" (107 cm)	**Height:** 4'1" (124 cm)
Weight: 45 lbs (20 kg)	**Weight:** 40 lbs (18 kg)	**Weight:** 57 lbs (26 kg)

Alexander, Tanner and Andrew were last seen on Thursday, November 25, 2010 at 2:30 pm at 112 East Congress. They may have been traveling with John Skelton in a dark Blue 2000 Dodge caravan Michigan registration 9JQ H93 up until 130pm on November 26th, 2010, both pictured below:

REWARD OFFERED OF UP TO $60,000 LEADING TO THE
RETURN/RECOVERY OF THE BOYS AND/OR TIPS LEADING TO
SUCCESSFUL PROSECTION OF THOSE RESPONSIBLE.

CALL MORENCI POLICE DEPARTMENT
AT (517) 458-7104

Wanted poster issued shortly after the boys came up missing.

Chapter 1

The Big Search

John Russell Skelton talked about his kids a lot after they disappeared.

They were all together on Thanksgiving Day, Nov. 25, 2010, at his house on 100 E. Congress St. in Morenci, Michigan. Neighbors saw the kids playing in his front yard at about 2:30 p.m. Tanner was 5 and he wore camouflage pajama pants with a Scooby Doo T-shirt. Alexander, 7, wore a gray T-shirt and black pajama pants. Andrew, 9, wore brown jammies with orange trim.

Skelton and his wife, Tanya Zuvers, were separated but they both lived in Morenci, four blocks apart. She was a stay-at-home mom taking college classes and he was a long-haul truck driver on the road a lot, or would have been if a DUI hadn't cost him his job the year before.

When Zuvers filed for divorce on the morning of Sept. 13, 2010, Skelton picked up the two oldest boys from school that afternoon and ran to his parent's house in Florida. She called 911 and Morenci Police Chief Larry Weeks responded. He got on the phone with Skelton and talked him down, then she drove down and picked them up. No charges were ever filed but Lenawee Circuit Court Judge Margaret Noe awarded sole custody to Tanya when they all got back.

Skelton was supposed to get the kids home by

The search for Andrew, Alexander and Tanner Skelton turned into a homicide investigation in January 2011. Morenci Police Chief Larry Weeks is shown making that announcement during a press conference. **Author photo**

8:30 a.m. the day after Thanksgiving, but Zuvers offered to pick them up early because "Something just wasn't setting right." When she called, Skelton told her he was at home but the kids were with his friend, Joanne Taylor, a pastor's wife in Jackson.

When Zuvers called a second time, Skelton said he was actually in a hospital in Toledo because he had tried to hang himself. That's when she called the police again.

Chief Weeks went down to Toledo and talked to Skelton in the hospital. Skelton said Taylor and her husband were very nice people and they had met on the road when he stopped to help them out a couple years ago and they'd been friends ever since. Facebook friends mostly – chats, memes; an occasional email to see how things are going.

Things weren't going well at all that Thanksgiving night, Skelton said. He decided to kill himself so he called Joanne to get the kids out of the house. She was supposed to pick up the boys and take them back down to Florida. She didn't really know the kids that well, or their grandparents at all, but driving 15 hours and 44 minutes with three little strangers to a stranger's house just wasn't that big a deal. Neither was John's life, apparently. She didn't try to talk him down or call 911. She just picked up the kids and said good bye. Forever. Have a nice death.

Weeks didn't buy that story and he issued an Amber Alert to find the kids.

Morenci Fire Chief Chad Schissler stepped up with 25 volunteers and they started searching vacant lots and parks throughout Morenci as well as the woods around it.

"We're all friends and neighbors and we can't stand to do nothing," firefighter Bill Foster said at the time.

Lenawee County sheriff's deputies searched the back roads north of the Ohio state line and Fulton County sheriff's deputies did the same on their side south of it. Park rangers at Harrison Lake State Park hit their trails and literally beat bushes.

Weeks got a warrant to search Skelton's Congress Street residence and seize his electronics. A frantic Zuvers met them there with her set of keys but police had to force their way in.

"John Skelton nailed a two-by-four across the door (on the inside)," she said. The house was busted up like a frat party gone bad. "There was broken dishes, things just thrown about, furniture broken and mattresses cut with a knife; dressers busted. I mean, there was just destruction everywhere."

The officer who popped the door open with a single kick is still her hero but John Skelton will always be John Skelton. She hasn't called him anything but that since the boys disappeared. He is not her husband or ex-husband or father of the boys any more. He's just a guy with a name.

===

On Monday, Nov. 29, Weeks went public with the findings from his warrant.

"We cannot say that Joanne Taylor does not exist, but we found no proof that John Skelton had a relationship with anyone by that name," Weeks said. Skelton's only Facebook activity was on his own wall, where he posted "May God and Tanya forgive me" late that Thursday evening.

It was Weeks' first formal press conference and he held it in the fire station's training room. Half the room was packed with friends, neighbors and volunteers standing shoulder-to-shoulder behind a picket fence of tripods with television cameras and fluffy-tipped microphones on sticks.

Weeks also said that Skelton's minivan, a blue Dodge Caravan with a missing gas cap, was "known to have driven from the Ohio Turnpike through Holiday City and West Unity Thursday evening."

The search, he said, was going to shift to that area.

The FBI already had two planes in the air with search and rescue dogs on the ground and a team of profilers set up shop in the police station's conference room. As news spread, more volunteers pitched in. They walked door-to-door. They stapled "Have you seen me?" posters on every telephone pole in Morenci and taped them to all the storefront windows on Main Street.

Skelton, still in the hospital, said he couldn't remember what happened to the kids, but he had a dream about them at the abandoned schoolhouse in Kunkle, Ohio. He also said that he remembered seeing a dumpster in the Ramada Inn parking lot in Holiday City. That was significant, he said, because in 2007 he wrote a poem about a little boy abandoned in a dumpster and what the kid thought about as he died.

Holiday City sits in the center of Williams County so the FBI sent a cadaver dog team to the county landfill where they sifted through the most recent layer of garbage. They also searched the old Kunkle schoolhouse. Nobody found anything.

===

After the press conference, 200 volunteers lined up inside the fire station and filed past the engines to sign up for search parties but organizing them was a slow process. They came dressed in layers, ready to spend the whole day outside. Within an hour they were down to T-shirts and their body odor out-stenched the smell of diesel fuel.

Cell phones blossomed with Tetris, Words With Friends, Candy Crush and Facebook posts. One hour stretched in to two and nothing happened. Boredom led to frustration and the crowd got loud.

Schissler was in the front office with his captains and lieutenants, scrubbing rosters to build 10-man teams with two firefighters in charge of each and they all had to be matched up with terrain and transportation. It was all high school algebra stuff nobody ever thinks they're going to use in real life: If a school bus can carry four search teams and it travels west on Morenci Road dropping one team at each intersection so they can walk two miles north to Mulberry Road, how many trips can the bus make before it has to start picking everybody up before dark? It was worse than that because once you cross U.S. 127 at the Hillsdale County line, Morenci Road turns in to Territorial Road and Mulberry Road turns in to Hartely Road. Seeley Road and Crowe Road run south from Hartely, but they don't connect to Territorial, and Lee Road runs north from Territorial, but it doesn't connect to Hartely. Hartely Road jags a half mile north of Mulberry so you have to add 30 minutes to the pickup times for those guys but Territorial doesn't run in a straight line anyway so who the hell knows when they'll be done?

Reporters like me roamed through the building with questions and cameras. We opened doors at annoyingly random intervals and the noise from the engine bay broke everyone's concentration in the front office. At the two hour mark, Schissler put firefighter Steve Miller in charge of crowd control because he was six-foot-six and a head taller than anybody else.

Miller cleared the hallway first. He told us we could work in the training room if we needed to or talk to people in the engine bay if we wanted to but we'd better "stay the hell out of the hallway."

Then he opened the side door to the engine bay and shouted "Keep it down!" No crowd ever just keeps it down for long so he did that a lot. People hushed when he walked in and roared when he walked out. Miller picked up on the pattern and finally figured out it was easier just to stay in the bay with the crowd.

He sat up a table and kept busy with paperwork, but most of the time he just walked around and answered questions. All of those questions were about why it took so long to get teams out the door and on the roads. Miller finally wrote on the wall, high up so everyone could see, "No one gets hurt. No one gets lost. No one gets left behind."

He pointed to that a lot.

===

Weeks wanted to expedite five teams and have them walk through the Lazy River Campground north of Holiday City that day but there were another 200 volunteers standing by at the Community Center in Pioneer, Ohio, just south of the state line. They were closer but they also needed to be organized and accounted for. Pam Carpenter, a full-time housewife and mother of two from Morenci, volunteered to make the drive and run the rosters by herself.

"It's overwhelming," she said, "but it's a blessing, really. It's what small towns do for each other."

The Pioneer crowd was mostly quiet. Those who didn't go to the campground stood outside watching the FBI planes circle in clover-leaf patterns around town. They also broke out their cell phones. It was the first day of deer season in Ohio and everybody knew somebody out in the woods.

"That really complicates things," Pioneer Police Chief Tim Livengood said. He was worried somebody was going to get shot. He was also worried about processing evidence. The entire north half of Williams County was a potential crime scene so every glove, rag and scrap of trash was about to be collected and analyzed. Whatever the hunters left behind was going to be mixed in and slow down the entire process.

===

Cambridge Township Fire Chief Scott Damon led one of the first search teams out of Morenci. They also went to Pioneer and walked south along Ohio 15, towards Holiday City.

"We really don't know what we're looking for," he said. "The word we got from law enforcement is that (Skelton) may have dumped the kids somewhere along the route. We're looking for any kind of evidence that will assist authorities."

A half mile later the whole team stopped and huddled up on the side of the road where somebody set up a hot chocolate stand at the Pioneer village limit.

Damon's team covered seven miles that afternoon. They walked five miles to Ohio Turnpike Exit 13 in Holiday City and another two miles to Ace Corners at Ohio 107, east of Montpelier.

I don't know why that intersection has its own name but it's always been that way. It's just a stop light with a car dealership and a trucking company on the east side of Ohio 15, and a gas station on the west. There's an empty woodlot on the northwest corner, and that's where Damon's team found a hole. "Looks like a shallow grave," he said.

Livengood came down and linked up with Williams County sheriff's deputies to cordon off the area.

A half hour later, two FBI agents showed up in a black SUV with a big bag of stuff. An Associated Press photographer pulled up right behind them and whipped out his thigh-sized telephoto lens and watched them probe the site for an hour.

When everybody else left the scene, he smiled and said "Up for a walk? Nobody's here to say we can't."

The hole did look like a shallow grave, roughly two feet wide, 3 feet deep and four feet long. The dirt pile next to it was still loose and damp and smelled fresh. No one knows who dug it or why and nobody ever found anything connecting it to the three boys.

===

Firefighter Robert Kune of Cambridge Township, Michigan, center, led a search team in Williams County on Nov. 29, 2010. As he huddled over maps on the hood of his truck near the Holiday City Ramada Inn, a local TV station reported the boys had been found across the street behind the Holiday Inn Express. They were wrong. Photo courtesy of The Bryan Times.

Cambridge Township firefighter Robert Kune led the search around Holiday City on Tuesday.

"Same plan as yesterday," he said, huddling over the map spread out on the hood of his pickup truck in the Ramada Inn parking lot. "We're just covering ground."

He started out with 60 people split into three big teams because they were going to cover the golf course at the Hillcrest Country Club east of Montpelier. Everybody was going to walk on line at double-arm intervals and sweep back and forth.

The first pass was easy. They walked with the wind at their backs and ignored the rain. They were happy; strolling along looking all over and chatting it up. When they spun around and the rain smacked them in the face they hunched into it with their heads down and straight forward. Nobody said a word.

They marched like that for three hours and went back to the Ramada Inn parking lot for lunch where Ann Slater, senior human resources manager for Kamco Industries Inc. in West Unity, delivered pizzas.

Kune and his team leaders did a working lunch with the map for a tablecloth; plotting, pointing, talking with their mouths full. The volunteers stood in clusters, wrapped around whoever had a smartphone with an internet connection.

They found out Skelton was out of the hospital and in custody at the Lucas County Jail in Ohio but he was going to be extradited back to Michigan. He also started changing his story – it wasn't Joanne Taylor who had the kids, it was a man named Niles with a woman named Sue. Maybe it was a guy named Elijah. He finally settled on no name at all. It was just a man in a van from a secret organization dedicated to protecting kids like his from mothers like theirs.

Weeks, in his morning press conference from Morenci, said Skelton would be charged with parental kidnapping. He said that sounded very optimistic, but he wasn't.

"We don't anticipate a positive ending," Weeks said.

A television reporter asked how Tanya Zuvers took the news and Weeks snapped. "This is every parent's worst nightmare. How would you deal with it?"

Another television station broke the story about Zuvers being a registered sex offender. This story, which aired on Nov. 29, 2010, was reported on WNWO-TV (NBC network) Channel 24 out of Toledo and was titled *Mom of missing Mich. boys on sex-offender list.*

In 1998, during her first marriage, she pled guilty to a fourth-degree misdemeanor charge of criminal sexual conduct because she had an affair with a 14-year-old boy her husband had hired to help take care of a rental property. Skelton used that during their divorce proceedings to argue that she was a threat to her own kids.

A TV station out of Detroit reported the boys had been found in Holiday City, behind another hotel right across the street from the Ramada Inn, earlier that morning.

Kune knew that was wrong. He said they would have been the first to find out. He even called Schissler and verified that the report was bogus, but people still left. They started checking out one and two at a time. Kune stood by his truck and stayed polite. He shook hands with every one of them. He told them he appreciated what they had done and he understood why they were leaving. He also pledged "to go it alone" if he had to because he knew the kids were still out there.

When Weeks heard that teams were falling apart he rushed to Holiday City and held another press conference from the back of Kune's pickup truck. "Somebody posted something on Facebook and the media ran with it," he said. "That is not the case at all." The boys were still missing and still out there somewhere, but it was too late. People were too cold and too wet and the search lost momentum.

That night the Rev. Ron Evans held a prayer vigil at the Kunkle United Brethren Church, three blocks east of the abandoned school house Skelton talked about. On Wednesday morning he walked into the Kunkle Fire Department and volunteered. He was a volunteer dispatcher for years after that, until he retired in 2017.

In Morenci, the firefighters' wives teamed up with church ladies and worked shifts through the night. They had hot biscuits and gravy ready for a thousand people before dawn.

===

So many people showed up Wednesday morning that Schissler had to park all of his fire apparatus outside.

It was chaos until firefighter Steve Miller waded into the crowd and bellowed like an Army drill sergeant. "Every team has a firefighter and the

More than 500 volunteers stepped up to search for Alexander, Andrew and Tanner Skelton in 2010. They spent seven days covering the 80-square-mile search area, most of which was in Williams County. Photo courtesy of The Bryan Times.

firefighter's in charge," he shouted. "No sightseeing and no independent searches. You don't want to search the way we do? Go home!"

It took another two hours to sort everyone out with Schissler and his officers building all new team rosters and bus manifests.

Brady Township firefighter Jarret Funk, from West Unity, was seriously frustrated. He sat against the wall in his turnout gear, staring at the crowd. "It's going to be a long day at this rate," he said. He worked third shift at Auto Farm Tool and Machine, in Fremont, Indiana, Tuesday night. After work, he drove 37 miles to Morenci, right past his own house without stopping. He waited two hours at the station for a 19-mile bus ride back to Pioneer (past his house again) so he could walk with a team before his next shift back in Fremont.

"It's all about closure for the family," Funk said. "I got four kids, 9, 7, 6 and 4. This just hits too close to home."

Lenawee County Sheriff's Deputy Jeff Peterson followed Funk's team back into Ohio and thanked them for being there.

"Walking the roads is the best way for us to use volunteers," Peterson said. "They can cover a lot of area and that frees us up to respond to tips and track down leads ... There have been a lot of tips since last Friday."

Incomplete geo-location data from John Skelton's cell phone led investigators to create and 80-square-mile search area in 2010. "You could hide a big pink ball in there and spend your whole life looking for it," Larry Weeks said afterward. He was the Morenci Police Chief and lead investigator for three years. Photo courtesy of The Bryan Times.

Volunteer search teams covered roadways and open areas during the 2010 search for Andrew, Alexander and Tanner Skelton. Every scrap they collected was taken in to evidence and analyzed. The boys remain missing to this day. Photo courtesy of The Bryan Times.

All of the teams hit the road that day because there were 80 square miles of road to cover. It was a box between Morenci, Pioneer, Holiday City and West Unity. They split down the middle and walked the asphalt with five people on each side. They spread out across ditches and into fields. They ducked into culverts and picked up trash – pop cans, beer cans, cigarette butts and anything that might have somebody's DNA on it. They bagged it, tagged it and marked with an orange flag so guys like Peterson could drive by, pick it up and turn it in to the Michigan State Police crime lab in Lansing for analysis.

Volunteers with a search and rescue dog covered the woods around the Lazy River Campground, where the Skelton family reportedly used to spend their vacations. Photo courtesy of The Bryan Times

The search area was still full of holes, though, because no one was searching on private property. In his Wednesday morning press conference, Weeks asked people to "walk their own estates" and report anything out of the ordinary. He started holding back a strategic reserve so at least one team was always ready to search a property as soon as the owner gave consent.

===

Thursday morning, Dec. 2, was different, more urgent, because Weeks wanted the main effort focused back on the Lazy River Campground. "It's an area of interest based on new information," he said in his press conference.

Angola firefighters from the Steuben County Underwater Rescue and Recovery Team used sonar to scan the St. Joseph River near the Lazy River Campground during the search for Andrew, Alexander and Tanner Skelton. The water had been shallow enough for deer to walk across the night before. The sonar picked up their tracks. Photo courtesy of The Bryan Times

That made Schissler's job a lot easier. He had 500 volunteers stacked in the engine bay, but half of them were going to the same place at the same time and they'd be there all day. He pushed everybody out the door in less than an hour.

Twelve buses went to the campground and volunteers swept over it like Kune's team did on the golf course Tuesday morning.

Another team, firefighters with engines, boats and divers, focused on three fishing ponds and the

St. Joseph River.

"It's really just a shot in the dark," diver Dennis Wisniewski said. "We're focusing on this area because of cell phone triangulation and the fact that someone saw Skelton's vehicle exit the Turnpike (in Holiday City). That's really all we have to go on so far."

The sky was clear, but it was bitterly cold so Wisniewski and the other divers stayed out of the water and used side scan sonar.

"It's a lot faster and easier than it used to be," Wisniewski said. He is a retired high school English teacher from Bryan, Ohio, but he's built like Marvel Comics' Wolverine – five-foot-eight and barrel-chested with a booming voice. When his church does plays, he always gets to be Satan and he makes the most of it.

He also has a passion for scuba diving, which has kept him involved with search and rescue teams for 32 years. Before sonar, they did underwater searches by hand, crawling underwater through mud and weeds. Reach. Sweep. Crawl. Repeat.

"It was cold, miserable work," he said. "You usually touch the bodies before you see them. This way, (with sonar) if we find something, it's a short dive in and out to retrieve it."

They found nothing and retrieved nothing on Thursday.

"Nothing but logs," Angola Fire Captain Bill Harter said, shaking his head as he climbed out of his boat on the St. Joe.

They also searched two gravel pits in the area and two retention ponds in Holiday City, one behind the Chase Brass and Copper Company and another behind the Ramada Inn.

John Skelton, at the Lucas County Jail, finally lawyered up and stopped talking all together.

===

Darwin and Shirley Krill, from Edgerton, Ohio, were among the first to show up in Morenci Friday morning. "We have four grandchildren and three of them are the same age as these kids," Shirley said. "We had to come. We just couldn't stay home."

Weeks, in his morning conference, said Friday would be the last day for volunteers and the end of search parties. Firefighter Steve Miller walked slowly through the crowd and talked quietly but that had nothing to do with Weeks' announcement.

"Every night we get together and figure out how to do things better," Miller said. He had 230 volunteers in the engine bay Friday morning, and that was a snap compared to the five- and six-hundred earlier in the week. They were out the door in less than 45 minutes.

At 4 p.m., with everybody coming back in, another team leader pushed for clearance to leave. Five firefighters had rounded up some late arrivals and got a search area assigned from Schissler. It was the last team on the last day with two hours of daylight, but Miller pointed to his board and lit into the guy for rushing through his rosters. "We don't cross out names," he said, shoving it back into the guy's hands. "Give me a clean copy of who's on the bus and never do it this way again."

That team got back three hours later and after dark, and Miller was pacing the floor like they were his teenage daughter until he could close out the report and wipe the stats off his white board. No one got lost. No one got hurt. No one got left behind.

There was no press conference after that, no speech, not even a prayer. Worn out volunteers simply got in their cars and left. Miller walked into the training room and looked at us in the press pool. All he said was "You can go now."

He and the other firefighters stayed late and cleaned the bay.

They sat up a row of tables in the middle for one more meeting. They didn't talk about what they did or what they could have done better. Most didn't talk at all. They raided the crock pots and roasters and ate dinner with their wives.

Weeks went home and ate with his family for the first time since their Thanksgiving dinner. He spent the weekend poring over data, looking at who went where, what they reported and what it all meant.

"It's a box of puzzle pieces," he said afterward. "Some of the pieces are missing and pieces from other puzzles are mixed in."

Skelton stayed at the Lucas County Jail but he had visitors. His parents came up from Florida and two ministers stopped by. He didn't tell them anything.

John Skelton

Chapter 2

Jackson Was Just too Close

Morenci Police Chief Larry Weeks never expected a positive outcome in the search for Andrew, Alexander and Tanner Skelton, but he held off on calling the search a homicide investigation until mid-February. He was waiting for a snow day because he wanted to make sure the kids who knew the brothers would be home with their families when the story came out.

He broke the story himself with another press conference in the fire department's training room as an east wind blew in ten inches of snow from Lake Erie. He apologized for the inconvenience but also explained that he didn't really need to. "The people of this town are my concern but you are not," he told the media afterward. "Be safe driving home." None of us complained.

It's still a homicide investigation but John Skelton has never been charged with murder. In July, 2011, he copped a plea in Lenawee County Circuit Court and pled no contest to three counts of unlawful imprisonment, which the Michigan Penal Code defines as "knowingly restraining a person to keep the location of confinement a secret."

Judge Margaret Noe found him guilty and hit him with a 15-year prison sentence. She broke it down to five years for each child because "taking them from their mother and all they've ever known is the cruelest from of imprisonment imaginable."

Weeks said the judge had to release more information than they wanted because she had to justify the harsh sentence. She said that while volunteers were out searching for the boys, Skelton told investigators things like "They'll hibernate until they graduate." She said they also found that Skelton had Googled things like "how to break a neck" and "does rat poison kill people" a week before the kids disappeared. He gave their coats and toothbrushes to another family member with instructions to never give them back to Zuvers. He said he didn't want her to have anything to remember them by.

After sentencing, Skelton started out at the Parnall Correctional Facility in Jackson, 44 miles northwest of Morenci and home of the apparently fictitious Joanne Taylor.

"Police wanted to keep him close so they could contact and question him easier, but that didn't go so well," Zuvers said. "Lots of people from Morenci are incarcerated up there and a few work as guards."

One day Chief Weeks told her Skelton had been moved to the Bellamy Creek Correctional Facility in Iona, in the western half of the state 125 miles away, but he never said why.

"I found out from Brewer (the Michigan State Police Detective Jeremy Brewer who took over the case in 2013) that he got the shit beat out of him," Zuvers said.

It was worse than that, she said, just like the shower scene in "The Shawshank Redemption."

"They took him to the hospital and had him sewn

up but when they took him back to his cell it happened again," she said. "They moved him to Iona because Jackson was just too close. He's still in protective custody up there. I used to get a burr under my saddle and post rants on Facebook. I'd post his address and ask people to write him, tell him what a piece of shit he was but I don't do that anymore. They moved him to keep him alive until they can find answers and I didn't really need to know that."

John Skelton has never given up any answers.

"That's the really creepy part," said Williams County Sheriff Steve Towns, who started his career as a corrections officer. "Everyone talks in prison. They either break down under interrogation or they brag to a buddy, but this guy has never said a word."

In 2012 John Walsh of "America's Most Wanted" picked up the Skelton brothers' story with an hour-long documentary called "Abduction in the Heartland." Photo courtesy of The Bryan Times.

Chapter 3

John Walsh Joins the Search

John Walsh of "America's Most Wanted" picked up the Morenci story in 2012 with an hour-long documentary called "Abduction in the Heartland."

Somehow my newspaper got exclusive access to his sound stage at the Hilton Garden Inn Conference Center in Perrysburg, Ohio, and I spent 45 minutes on the set with Walsh and Weeks, who was obviously not comfortable with stage makeup, before the on-camera interviews.

"I wish I could water board that son-of-a-bitch," Walsh said. "Just ten minutes alone to beat the shit out of him."

Weeks smiled and said "During the search, at the Morenci office, tensions were running high. Somebody suggested we water board him and one of the FBI agents in the back of the room raised his hand and said 'I'm certified, if anybody's interested.' We didn't do anything like that, of course, but it lightened the mood when we needed it."

Walsh nodded and smiled but he turned grim and started talking about his son Adam, who was abducted from a Sears department store in Florida and murdered on July 27, 1981.

"That two weeks when we didn't know where he was were the worst in my life," Walsh said. "The only thing worse was when they found his severed head.

"Whatever happened to these kids, we have to find out," Walsh said. "The family is never going to give up hope, but this has to end. The not knowing just kills you inside. It rips the heart of you forever. Dead or alive, they have to know. That's why we want to put the white hot spotlight on it."

The whole point behind his "Abduction in the Heartland" episode was that "John Skelton isn't the only one who knows what happened," Walsh said. "That's my gut feeling. Either he killed them and somebody saw something, or he's a cunning liar and he sent them underground with the help of family or friends."

Walsh picked up the story to generate tips because that's worked in the past. Anonymous tips called into the "America's Most Wanted" hotline (1-800-CRIMETV is still active, by the way) helped find 60 children alive, including Elizabeth Smart. She was abducted in 2002 and held captive for nine months.

"We found her when the FBI and no one else could," Walsh said. "Brian David Mitchell (her abductor) was even arrested and in jail for a weekend while she was missing. Every time we think we've got it figured out, somebody does something crazy that nobody's ever seen before."

Smart was found by someone who had watched AMW, spotted her the next morning and called police. During its 25 years on Fox, AMW tips have led to the arrest of 1,200 criminals in 13 countries; 17 of them were on the FBI's Most Wanted list.

"Somebody knows something," Walsh said again. "If they're afraid to call the police, they can call us.

They know we don't track the calls. All we need is that one tip."

===

"Abduction in the Heartland" aired nationwide on June 13, 2013, and the Australian-based "Crime Watch Daily" picked up the story and aired its episode on Oct. 9, 2015, on Fox channels.

Both shows still generate tips from re-runs and online videos. "Several times a week," according to Brewer.

"We still get tips from all over the country, 36 states so far," Brewer said in a phone interview on Nov. 11, 2015. "The Center for Missing and Exploited Children pushed out age-progression photos and we get calls from people who have seen boys that look like those. Usually three boys with parents acting weird. Every tip gets tracked down. We haven't found any solid evidence yet but that doesn't mean it won't happen in the future.

"It's still the biggest case in the state," Brewer said. "We keep plugging away on a daily basis. Any new information we get, we're all over it. Hopefully, one of these days it will pan out for us."

Some of those tips have led back to northwest Ohio.

Brewer confirmed they searched an area in Williams County in 2015 "but nothing ever came of it." I called Towns right after he said that to find out what happened. Towns said that search was in July and they sent a cadaver dog through a vacant house.

"We're still working it. We talk (with Brewer) several times a year and whenever we get a pinpointed area of interest we send somebody to check it out," Towns said.

"We'd like to coordinate a comprehensive search based on cell phone data, but manpower is always an issue," Towns said. "It's hard getting all the right pieces together at the right time."

Finding the right place for that comprehensive search is also a problem. The cell phone data collected on Nov. 26, 2010 is maddeningly vague.

Chapter 4

Puzzles

If every missing persons case is a puzzle, Holiday City may be the puzzle capital of Ohio.

For starters, it isn't much of a city. It's Exit 13 on the Ohio Turnpike with two restaurants, two gas stations, a Hudson Leather Factory Outlet store and no stop lights. It also has two hotels and two motels (The difference is in the doors: hotel room doors open into a hallway. Motel room doors open into a parking lot).

The village was named after its largest hotel, a Holiday Inn conference center that got renovated into a Ramada Inn before 2010 and then a Quality Inn after. There's a brand new Holiday Inn Express a block south of the Turnpike, so the village name is still legit.

Holiday City incorporated with 52 permanent residents in 1997 and since then five people (9.6 percent of the total population) have disappeared in the area. Toledo is the closest big city, with a population of 282,000. If 9.6 percent (27,072) of those people disappeared over the same time period, the Great Lakes Triangle would be more famous than the one in Bermuda.

===

Mary Kozier was the first to disappear, on Dec. 7, 2000. "She was a motel clerk at the Econo

Lodge," said Al Word, who was Williams County sheriff at the time. He said the people who owned the place also lived there and when they got home at 1 a.m. she wasn't there. They found an empty cash drawer from the register sitting on the counter and they saw that she had sent a fax less than an hour before. It was nothing special, just a room bill.

Al Word

"I knew it was gonna be bad," Word said. "It was cold that night, but her purse and her coat were still there." He broadcast an ATL (Attempt To Locate bulletin) with Kozier's description to every police department in Williams County and sent his deputies out to search the county roads around Holiday City.

Jeff Arnold was a police detective back then and he was pushing out his own ATL for two guys who had just robbed the Sterling convenience store at 923 S. Main St. in Bryan, nine miles south of Holiday City. The clerk called 911 and said one of them was a "skinny white guy" and the other was a "big black guy." They wore masks and they had a shotgun and they took $400. He saw their vehicle but he couldn't get a license plate number.

"I was on duty that night and I'd just foot-chased a kid across town," said James Snively, who was a patrolman in Bryan at the time. "I was still cold and wet when the robbery call came in."

Pioneer Police Officer Jeff Priester heard both ATLs. He knew the car Arnold was talking about and probably one of the guys in it.

Pioneer is four miles north of Holiday City but not much bigger. It has four stop lights but they're all at the same crooked intersection where Baubice Street wraps around two sides of the local library. The Pizza Barn stands right next to the library and the North Central High School is three blocks east. So many students cut class for lunch that the Board of Education finally decided to let them deliver on campus.

James B. Jones and Jason Lamar Crawford both attended Pioneer's North Central High School. Both were from Toledo and both moved into local foster homes. Crawford graduated in 1998 and moved back to Toledo. Jones dropped out in 1999 and followed him. He moved back to Pioneer a couple months later after a drug offense and went through rehab. He had a child of his own and he wanted to make things right.

Priester played a hunch and started driving extra loops around Jones' neighborhood. When Jones and Crawford pulled up in front of a friend's house at 3 a.m., Priester found a shotgun in the back seat with a mask and jacket that matched Arnold's ATL.

By 5 a.m., Jones and Crawford were back in Bryan at the police station.

"I was sitting with the younger gentleman (Jones) and we heard somebody in the hallway talking about their car," Snively said. "I saw his whole demeanor change so I just kind of casually said 'Hmmm, I wonder what's in there?' That's when he asked to talk to Arnold."

Arnold picked up the narrative from there. "Jones was scared," Arnold said. "He knew we had him on the Sterling robbery and he was probably just as scared of Crawford as he was of us."

The Econo Lodge was their first stop, and probably their first-ever attempt at robbery, Arnold said, because neither of them had thought to wear masks. Kozier recognized Jones as soon as he walked in the lobby because she had been his Sunday school teacher when he first moved to Pioneer.

Jones told Arnold they forced Kozier into the trunk of their car and drove out to Opdycke Park, on County Road 16, halfway between Bryan and Holiday City. They took her down under the Beaver Creek bridge where Crawford shot her in the neck and watched her die. Then they went on to Bryan where they picked up a couple ski masks, hit the Sterling store and drove back to Pioneer.

"We stopped everything at that point and rushed out to find her," Arnold said.

Snively and officer Todd Snyder were first on the scene and Sheriff Word arrived minutes later.

"I found her," Snively said in a 2015 interview, slowly sipping his coffee. He wouldn't say anything more.

Word also refused to talk about what they found at the scene "but it still bothers me," he said when I talked to him more than 10 years later. "What we saw under the bridge, that's never going to go away ... You know she had ten grandkids, right? We found her knitting needles under the counter. It was close to Christmas and she was making them stuff ... All they got was $181 from the register.

"It was good police work all around, especially Priester," Word said. "He broke the case just being vigilant and perceptive like every cop should be."

Snively said "All the Bryan third-shift guys chipped in and got him a steak dinner."

===

When Al Word retired his Chief Deputy, Kevin Beck, ran unopposed as the next sheriff and he tapped Snively as his chief deputy. Both were in the sheriff's office when the Skelton brothers disappeared in 2010 and they were still there two years later when a 48-year-old truck driver from New Hampshire disappeared from the Ramada Inn across the street from Kozier's Econo Lodge. Surat Nuenoom was reported missing on March 16, 2012, after failing to deliver goods in Gary, Indiana.

Deputies tracked his credit card and found that he had checked into the hotel at 7 p.m. the night prior. His rig was still in the parking lot and his personal effects, including a wallet and two cell phones, were still in his room. A couple witnesses reported seeing a male subject hitch hiking on a county road that same night and Beck's initial press release said "No foul play is suspected at this time."

On March 20, Beck dispatched a team of

volunteer divers with a Humminbird side-scan sonar to search the retention pond behind the hotel. "We have no reason to believe he's in there," he said at the scene. "No tips, no information. We just want to clear the pond and make sure, because it's so close to the hotel." I was there and stood next to Beck on shore throughout the search.

On May 7, 52 days later, David Tomaszewski and Russell Sutton found Nuenoom's body.

"We hadn't been here more than 30 minutes," Tomaszewski said, standing outside the circle of police tape wrapped around the same spot where I had stood with Beck in March. "We thought it was a log or tree stump at first, but it really looked like a body so I walked over and checked it out."

"He had gray hair, blue jeans, a jean jacket and boots," Sutton added. "We're never going to fish here again!"

On May 11, Williams County Coroner Dr. Kevin Park confirmed it was Nuenoom. He said the cause of death was drowning and estimated the time of death to be on or about March 16, the same day Nuenoom was reported missing by his boss. He also said it appeared to be a suicide.

===

After the Nuenoom search, I reasoned that if one diver with hi-tech sonar can miss a large adult body, it's probably just as easy for another to miss three smaller ones in the same pond so I started working on an investigative report.

Beck said he purchased the sonar for his divers

earlier that year "because we saw it in action during the search for the three boys from Morenci." His volunteer divers accompanied the Steuben County Underwater Rescue and Recovery Team (SCURRT) from the Angola, Indiana, Fire Department during the search.

It was a good intention but there were budgetary limitations.

"I remember those guys," said Dennis Watters, the CEO of Team Watters Sonar Search and Rescue Inc., when I called his office in Moro, Illinois.

"They got a $4,000 system but they didn't get the training package to go with it," Watters said.

The money just wasn't there, according to Beck's dive team leader, Dennis Wisniewski, who spoke during the Skelton search.

"The company offered to send a rep, but it would have cost $500 for a one-day class," he said. "We worked with Angola a little bit. They showed us stuff because they had the system before we did."

Beck said his divers "showed a lot of initiative" because they set the system up from the instruction manual and learned to use it by searching for golf balls in Wisniewski's backyard pond.

But using the system isn't the same as understanding how it works.

"The problem is that not every body looks like a body," Watters said. "You have to look at what doesn't belong to be more successful. The settings are everything, ninety percent of the battle if you do it right. The other 10 percent is interpretation."

"My first search is a classic example," Watters

said. "It wasn't a slam dunk. On sonar it looked like anything but a body and, to be perfectly honest, we missed it on the water. We had to go back, re-look and re-see everything. We found it on the play-back ... It could have been something as simple having eyes focused on the wrong side of the screen at the time."

It happened again in 2008, even after a career's worth of experience, while searching for a drowning victim in St. Taminy Parish, Louisiana. "We clearly had him," Watters said. "We missed him on the water and found him on the laptop. Totally clear, like he was photo shopped. We went out and recovered him the next day ... That first contact, it's never 'Here I am, come and get me.'

"One search we found four kids," Watters said. "Three of them looked just like rocks, but the texture was different. We knew they were in there and the texture was just different enough to investigate. Every image is subject to interpretation. When you're at depth and you've had a lot of practice, you completely re-think a body.

"People think when you drown you sink like a rock but that's not the case," Watters said. "They can be standing, hovering, sitting ... Sometimes they just look really weird. We went to one where the guy had a cinder block tied to him and the block floated within two hours. We've had three where they were standing up, suspended off the bottom just a little bit. It's the air in their pockets that does it and it's the most eerie image you ever want to see."

Watters said the Humminbird sonars are "popular in the Midwest" where ponds and streams tend to be shallow, but shallow water has its own set of variables.

"Whatever the sound hits first, it returns with that image," Watters said. "Grass makes sonar ineffective. Sound hits the top of the grass and returns so all you might get is a hole. It's the same with a ledge or a log. If you're 50 feet away the acoustic shadow gives you an incredible image of the log but nothing behind it. If you miss it by an inch it might as well be a mile."

In 20 feet or less, a simple Humminbird sonar is good enough to find a body, but deeper than 25 feet you need a Marine Sonic system behind the boat just off the bottom. "We would have used both at once if we were there," Watters said. "If we see something with the Humminbird we mark it right there so you don't need any math to figure it out. The Marine Sonic has a set back because of the cable length, but together they can provide two angles of the same image.

"We recovered a car from in Alton, Illinois, once," Watters said. "Police had this guy in video, driving right into the Mississippi River. They searched the area three times with a towed sonar ten feet off the bottom and never found anything. The problem was that it was an old dam site and they were passing right over. We picked it up from the surface looking straight down into the hole. They weren't bad guys; their system just wasn't hitting it, skimmed right over the top.

"And we don't declare anything without two

scans, one going north-south and another going east-west, all with super high definition imagery," Watters said. "A lot of it is about experience and time behind the screen because that first contact is never 'Here I am, come and get me.'"

Almost never. His fastest recovery was 1 minute, 48 seconds. "We were asked to help with a drowning victim and police happened to be talking about a car that disappeared years ago," Watters said. "We found the car right after we put in at the boat dock. They blew it off at first, but boom! It was right there.

"We fish with ours just about every day," Watters said.

When he's not working search and rescue missions you can probably find him at a bass fishing tournament in Texas, because success with one leads to success with the other. "It's all about seat time on the water, always up on what works and what doesn't, figuring out the glitches in new software and keeping up with the upgrades on whatever system you got," Watters said.

He also said that Humminbird had issued a systems upgrade early in 2010. Volunteer organizations that don't use the system until it's needed probably never knew.

===

Angola Fire Lt. Bill Harter led the SCURRT divers during their 2010 search for the Skelton brothers in Williams County. His team searched the Holiday City retention pond, the three ponds on the Lazy River Campground, the St. Joseph River and several farm ponds on private property when the owners consented.

When I submitted a Freedom of Information Act request for Harter's sonar data he was more than happy to cooperate. He redacted all of the locations to protect the integrity of the law enforcement investigation, but he said "We're drowning focused, not homicide focused. If we missed something we'll go back there in a heartbeat."

My paper had that data peer-reviewed by Watters and Gene Ralston, a sonar operator who works underwater surveys for the United States Geological Service and uses the same systems to assist in FBI investigations.

Watters lives in Illinois and he watched the search unfold on TV. "We were contacted by several people and relatives when the search was hot and heavy, but we never got the blessing of the investigating agency," he said. "You can't just butt in and you just don't show up until you get officially asked by law enforcement or a fire department. If you don't get that blessing you get locked out."

I found Ralston in Idaho through Google searches. He had no knowledge of the 2010 search and never heard about the Skelton case, but as soon as he got the images he shot back "this probably came from a local team using Humminbird." He also stressed, repeatedly, that his comments "weren't meant to be critical of any operator" and "I'm not being critical at all and I don't want my comments to be taken that way."

Then Ralston said he "wouldn't be at all

surprised" if a body was missed.

"I did an image review of a drowning in a lake near Cincinnati once and the Ohio Department of Natural Resources uses the same sonar system we do," Ralston said. "We reviewed the images and saw the father and son right away. They argued it was woody debris and never went back to the lake. We re-scanned and reviewed everything again and saw them even clearer, almost perfect. The family paid us to come recover the bodies and we did.

"The family asked how that could happen, but the truth is it just does," Ralston said. "I've recovered 80 bodies and I've missed a few ... It just happens sometimes ... People think it works like a magnet, you put it in the water and get them but that's not true. It's all in the difference between what you're looking *at* and what you're looking *for.*

"Humminbird is not a true sonar," Ralston said. "It will ping and listen, ping and listen. It's not continuous. It's good for shallow water searches but really, it's just a glorified fish finder."

That ping-and-listen cycle limits boat speed, Ralston said. "If you go too fast, you'll miss details. Speed needs to be about 2 miles per hour to make seamless images. Any faster and the images will melt into one another – the third image will lay on top of the first and skip the second."

Harter's boat speed during the 2010 search is unknown. That information was also redacted.

High-tech systems work great, but complex machines are easily affected by variables, Ralston said. "Sonar has a lot of variables. You're just not proficient if you don't use it very often. I did an FBI case where they searched a whole lake for a 55-gallon drum. One team missed it then another came in and they found it within two hours."

The position of observers and their direction of travel also make a big difference. "If you travel parallel or perpendicular to an object, that changes the acoustic shadow," Ralston said. "It's like sunrise and sunset; longer shadows in different directions change the appearance of everything.

"We found twin brothers once, one was parallel to our direction of travel and the other was perpendicular," Ralston said. "One we found easy. The other took a lot longer and we didn't find him until his shadow gave him away. That's why you really have to understand how sounds make images."

Soil surface also makes a difference.

"Soft bottoms are perfect," Ralston said. "They absorb sound and that makes objects stand out. Hard bottoms don't. They wash out everything and you have to set the gain way, way low to see the difference. You've got to look for the shadows, not the body."

A recently-dredged pond would be a hard surface with little debris and a river bank would be soft with lots of debris. SCURRT covered both types during their search in 2010. I tried to get the Holiday City retention pond's original dig permit and design specs from the county engineer's office to find out what its bottom was like but that didn't take a lot of time. Engineer Dennis Bell said it was "just a hole in the ground meant to hold water."

The fact that the sonar was attached to the boat

during the search also made a difference, Ralston said. "We tow our sonar behind, away from the boat. The key is to get the source of the sound as close to the bottom as you can. We try to get 10 to 15 feet off the bottom, low-angle illumination like a sunrise so the features and shadows are very vivid."

Using a boat-mounted sonar "is like high-noon and it washes everything out," Ralston said. The bottom line is "you have to know what to look for and what to look at a second time, from different angles and different directions."

Ralston also said that "It's not unreasonable for a novice to find a body because they probably have an image in mind for what they're looking for; a stereotypical image of what a body looks like, but a lot depends on having an open mind for what you're looking for."

The brothers would not have looked like bodies on sonar, Ralston said. "They were most likely packaged; most intentional body disposals are. Nobody travels with bodies in a car and the (sonar) operator has to keep that in mind."

"In shallow water, bodies tend to rest on the bottom in a sitting position," Ralston said. "They'd look like a tree stump or a log on sonar. In deep water, unwrapped like with a drowning, bodies rest on their backs with arms up and knees bent. You'd see the shadows. The two spikes for the arms would make an 'A' and the legs would make a W."

On Nov. 21, 2015, The Times identified one of the "documented anomalies" in the 2010 SCURRT data that resembled Ralston's description. It looked

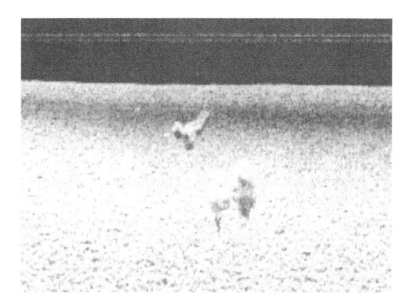

This image from sonar scans during a search of the St. Joseph River shortly after the Skelton boys' disappearance shows some of the markers that might indicate a body under water. Experts, however, would not confirm what the image actually shows.

like somebody doing one too many push-ups with arms bent at 90-degrees away from the torso and the person's legs resting on the floor. It was between four-foot-six-inches and five-feet long. Neither Ralston nor Watters could confirm what the image was.

Watters said it "looked just like a body, but it's probably woody debris."

Ralston said "I can't say what that thing is but it looks very suspicious ... Somebody should have done a dive on the thing to rule it out, one way or another."

That never happened. No one ever sent the

divers back because investigators never even saw the images.

The sonar reports, according to Weeks, were just reports like all the others. "Someone signed under oath that they searched a specific area at a specific time and date and didn't find a body," he said.

The Times contacted the Angola Fire Department again, to ask about that specific image, four days later. Fire Lt. Kevin Mory responded with "At this time the fire chief has advised that in order to comment on any pictures you will have to contact the city attorney."

The city attorney never returned our calls.

===

John Skelton's cell phone connected to the Holiday City cell phone tower on the same day the brothers disappeared and that tower is across the street from the retention pond where Nuenoom was found. Skelton could have been there, right there, and all I had to do was prove it.

I called on Josiah Harness, a retired Army Intelligence NCO who specialized in profiling human behavior. We were supposed be in Afghanistan in 2010 but our battalion was one of several that got "off ramped" that year.

He laughed when I explained my theory.

"Assuming the kids are there ... That would be a rookie mistake," Harness said. "This pond you talk about, it means something to you, right? You've put all kinds of time into checking out?"

"Not really," I lied.

"The problem is that (the pond) doesn't mean anything at all to this other guy," he said. "It's just a place on a map to him.

"The dude had a plan and very good one," Harness said. "I mean, it had to be a pretty good plan because nobody's ever found the kids, right? The good news is that all plans are predictable. People always fall back on routines and routines leave patterns."

"This guy's life was going to shit so he probably ran to his happy place, his favorite thinking spot," Harness said. "You just gotta figure out where that place was."

Skelton has never talked about where he went and probably never will so finding his happy place started with an entirely different set of pings.

John Skelton's phone "pinged" to this cell phone tower in Holiday City the day his sons disappeared. Author photo.

Chapter 5
Cell Phone Pings

At 1:22 a.m. May 10, 2015, the Williams County Communications Agency (WCCA) reported someone called 911 four times in a row and never said a word.

Emergency dispatchers accessed the signal data and found the calls came from a cell phone in Bryan. In less than a minute they determined the phone was at the Wal-Mart, 1215 S. Main St. They narrowed it down to the Lawn and Garden Center, then the checkout counter at the front door. When police arrived they found the phone belonged to a cashier and it was auto-dialing 911 in her pocket for no apparent reason. That is the power of Enhanced 911 and dispatchers like Kelly Buchanan have been using it since 2008.

"We can find anyone who calls," Buchanan said. "Sometimes we can even find them if they don't. If it's a big enough emergency, like a suicide attempt or an Amber Alert, we can ping their phones."

Dawn Baldwin is the WCCA director and Buchanan's boss. She explained that cellphones send out a "handshake" signal every couple of seconds to stay connected to the network. That signal includes the cell phone's number with its location by latitude, longitude and elevation. It bounces around every cell tower within reach. The network is always looking for the best handshake and it pushes calls through the cell tower with the best reception.

Remember the "Can You Hear Me Now" guy with the Buddy Holly glasses in the old Verizon commercials? The whole point was that Verizon cell phones sent handshake signals faster than most, so their calls were less likely to lose signal strength and get interrupted. His name is Paul Marcarelli. In 2011, he told The Atlantic that at his cousin's wedding more people took photos with him than the bride. That same year at his grandmother's funeral someone leaned up and whispered "Can you hear me now?" as her coffin was being lowered. (Morgan, 2014)

Handshake signals are always out there.

"As long as your phone has power, it will try to stay connected," Baldwin said. When her dispatchers do a ping, they trace the handshake signals backwards to find the source.

Pings are also part of the metadata the National Security Agency uses to track terrorists around the world and the Drug Enforcement Agency uses metadata in northwest Ohio to track drug dealers on the Ohio Turnpike. I pitched a story to my editor and spent a week trying to find out if anybody used cell phone metadata to find Andrew, Alexander and Tanner Skelton.

I found out they never even had access to it!

When police "pinged" John Skelton's cell phone all they got were the tower connections. At 4:29 a.m. it was connected to the Morenci cell tower. At 5:02 a.m., 33 minutes later, his phone connected to the Holiday City cell tower 31 miles away. At 6:46 a.m., 104 minutes later, it connected back to the

Morenci cell tower. The original search area in 2010 was 80 square miles because nobody ever got precise locations the metadata should have provided.

Those three pings were "based on what (John Skelton's) cell phone carrier provided," Jeremey Brewer said. He was involved in the investigation from Day One. He was a state police detective assigned to assist Weeks in 2010. He was sergeant assigned to the case when state police took the lead in 2013 and now, as a lieutenant, he leads the investigation. "Whenever we submit a warrant we get what we get," he said. "We're at the whim of what they provide.

"It's not an exact science but we go back through it quite often, every time there's new technology or new training. Checked. Double checked. Triple checked a thousand times," Brewer said. "We're always trying to glean more information. This is the biggest unsolved case in the state and the information is in somebody's hands every day."

===

There should have been more data than just three tower connections, said Kevin DeLong, the vice president of mobile forensics at Syntricate, a Cleveland-based company that specializes in technical support for cyber security and digital investigations. "That should raise eyebrows," he said. "It's odd there were only three pings, but it's hard to say why."

Part of the problem may be the source of

information. "When police have a warrant for data, they call the cell phone carrier's subpoena compliance hotline, but that is not the carrier," DeLong said. "They farm compliance out to legal types."

The Times also talked to digital forensic analyst Michael O'Kelly, the "Cell Tower Mike" who was an expert witness during the Casey Anthony trial in 2011. He said the same thing and more.

Mining cell phone data is a tedious process and that usually falls on entry-level employees. "Literally, they could have been flipping burgers the day before," O'Kelly said. "I spent 30 minutes arguing with one once because they didn't know what the word 'azimuth' meant."

Azimuth is an important term in mobile forensics. It is a specific direction based on degrees from a compass. General directions are too vague for precise measurements over long distances so south has to be an azimuth of 180-degrees exactly. A little east would be 179 degrees and a little west would be 181 degrees. One degree of difference stretched over a cell phone tower's seven-mile radius could be football fields wide.

DeLong said all of the "real information" would have been in the Network Operations Center that handles all of the switch logs for the Midwest from Mansfield, Ohio.

"Switch logs work like Internet routers for your laptop," DeLong said. They track cell phone locations and coordinate which towers their calls should be routed through for best reception.

"If you want the real information you need a

direct line to them," DeLong said. "The Secret Service does that and they have tools local law enforcement never knew existed."

Another part of the problem was time.

"Pings are usually right on the money but this wasn't one of those," DeLong said. The three pings from Skelton's cell phone weren't "live," he said. They came hours after the fact, after the kids were reported missing.

Stale metadata from Skelton's cell phone would not have been an exact GPS coordinate like a live ping, but it should have narrowed down the search based on his distance from the cell tower and which azimuth his phone's signal came from. That would have been recorded when it "touched the network," DeLong said. "It would have been a broad location based on tower feedback, probably as big as a couple city blocks, but still better than 80 square miles."

===

Skelton, as it turns out, had a Verizon cell phone just like Paul Marcarelli bragged about in 2010. (He changed sides in 2017 and started pitching for Sprint. He talks a lot of smack about Verizon now but that doesn't change the technology.)

Early in their divorce proceedings, Skelton agreed to pay for a cell phone family plan so everyone could stay in touch with the kids, according to Zuvers. He backed out within a couple weeks claiming he had inadequate funds but then "his mommy bought him a new one," she said.

Skelton's cell phone is still in evidence, so I borrowed one like it and Baldwin let me drive around for an hour making test calls to 911 while Buchanan was at the desk.

The first call was made on the fly, driving north on Ohio 15 at 55 miles per hour. Buchanan found the location, but it wasn't easy. Her first ping hit off a cell tower in Stryker. Her second ping hit off a tower on Fulton County Road H, in Franklin Township. After 45 seconds she said, "Gotcha. Oakwood trailer park," as I drove by it. A printout of the phone data afterward showed a 497-meter "circle of confidence." She knew I was inside that circle so she picked the biggest landmark.

I made a second call west of Kunkle, at County Road O and County Road 16, next to the Menards Distribution Center. It is one of the largest factories in Williams County with big metal buildings and big machines; satellite dishes and lots of people with cell phones. None of that stuff was there in 2010 so any cell phone signal in the area back then would have had a lot less interference. Buchanan pinged my phone on the first try and her circle of confidence was 25 meters.

I made my third call on U.S. 20, next to the Lazy River Campground where all of the search teams converged on Dec. 2, 2010. Buchanan pinged my phone again on the first try, with a 45-meter circle of confidence.

After the drive I asked Baldwin, if an Amber Alert was issued when the kids were reported missing and Skelton's cell phone touched the network through the Holiday City cell tower, why didn't anyone pick up a circle of confidence like we just did?

Baldwin didn't know. She was a dispatcher in 2010, not the agency director, but she had a guess. She ran to her bookshelf and leafed through the agency's "big book of protocols." She found the county had 16 cell towers in 2010. They were owned by Centennial, T-Mobile, Sprint, Nextel and Alltel. Verizon wasn't even on the list.

"Their technology hadn't been settled yet," Baldwin said. "All of their calls had to be passed through other companies."

That company would have been Alltel, O'Kelly said. They were a subsidiary of Verizon in 2010 and "that may be the game changer," he said. "If the files are anywhere, they'd be with Alltel ... It may end up with two engineers, one from each company, sifting through data to find it."

Finding specific metadata in an Alltel file won't be that easy, though.

Allied Wireless actually ran the cell network in Ohio in 2010. That was a subsidiary of Alltel, which became a subsidiary of Verizon in June 2008. But then in April 2010, seven months before the kids disappeared, Verizon divested parts of Alltel, sacrificing Allied Wireless to Atlantic Tele-Network. ATN passed Allied down to its subsidiary, Commnet Wireless LLC. Then, in January 2013, AT&T took over ATN and sacrificed Commnet Wireless to Sprint.

"All that may actually be good news in this case," O'Kelly said.

When Skelton's Verizon cell phone entered

territory covered by the Allied Wireless network its metadata became an Allied corporate asset, which may have been preserved during all of the merger negotiations from one carrier to another. "But there's always a chance they haven't saved it," O'Kelly said. "They may not have seen a need for it. Cell phone companies are all about making money tomorrow, not yesterday. Everything a carrier does is money oriented."

Even if Skelton's metadata is gone there is still a way to re-create it.

"The FBI tracks and records cell tower settings every day," O'Kelly said. "You could use that data to recreate the digital scene. The frequency is the key. Which one was it and who has it now? Get that and you can run tests all day long. The changes in technology from then to now won't even matter if you have that frequency."

But that also isn't as easy as it sounds.

Once the towers in question are re-set to frequencies from Nov. 26, 2010, investigators would need nearly identical weather. Leaves absorb cell phone signals and "Cell towers get re-tuned twice a year because of that," O'Kelly said. "Once when the leaves are on trees and again after they're off." Snow does the same thing. There was mild weather in November 2010 with hardly any snow, but most of the leaves had fallen.

Investigators would also have to drive Skelton's route in a 2000 Dodge Caravan exactly like his. The wires in the rear-window defroster could make a difference. So could the sunroof. The missing gas cap, maybe not so much.

Once the digital crime scene was recreated, all of the signals from Skelton's cell phone would have to be mapped and analyzed.

"Cell towers are like ink plots, not just a circle," O'Kelly said. "Sometimes there are extra dots, separated from center mass because of hills and valleys, but all that can tell you something. Even the dead space matters. Where was he when he got a signal? Where was he when he didn't and how long was he there?"

When I made my call from the Lazy River Campground, my phone actually hit off a cell tower on County Road 8, near Columbia. It was 12 miles away but the Holiday City tower was less than three. No one knows why, not even O'Kelly. Not yet. Cell phone forensics is an exact science, but there are a lot of variables.

Alexander, Tanner and Andrew Skelton

Age progression photos of Alexander, Tanner and Andrew Skelton distributed in 2016 by the Center for Missing and Exploited Children.

Chapter 6

Eighty Percent Sure

Odds are Andrew, Alexander and Tanner Skelton are still somewhere in Williams County but Kevin Beck has never said a word about it, at least not publicly.

"That case was really hard on him, a lot more than he ever let on," said Lisa Nye. She was the office clerk during Beck's administration as sheriff. "We were hoping we'd find them here in the county (because) Ohio has the death penalty but Michigan doesn't."

When the search and its media frenzy started "I offered to do joint press conferences (with Beck) but he was never interested," Larry Weeks said when I sat down with him in 2012. As a sheriff, whose job as an elected official depended on public opinion, Beck was "surprisingly passive," Weeks said.

Neither Beck nor anyone connected to him has ever explained why.

===

My dad spent 25 years as a tool and die maker at the Hayes-Albion auto parts plant in West Unity and in 1979 he had the second highest seniority. I still don't know what that means exactly, but that summer was the best I ever had. We shopped for ski boats and talked about getting a cottage. We flew out to Seattle for two weeks and I celebrated my tenth birthday on Mount Rainier. (I got car sick on the way down. My dad gave me his sweater and told me to aim for it so I wouldn't mess up Aunt Louise's car. It was a nice sweater so I splattered her back seat anyway. I had no idea he'd be cleaning up the mess.)

Hayes-Albion shut down about a month after that without warning. My dad went to work and all the doors were locked. He spent a lot of time at home after that and I had a blast! I got to run the Stanley Steamer carpet cleaner all by myself and paint the living room ceiling with a roller. Rollers are way more fun than brushes. We did a lot of manly-man projects around the house that fall. I didn't know my parents were planning to sell it until after I graduated from college 12 years later.

My dad found another factory job that winter and we kept the house but without seniority he got laid off a lot. He picked up a second job flipping burgers at the Turnpike Plaza north of West Unity and my mom starting working at my uncle's pizza shop in Montpelier. I loved that too because my cousin knew how to get free games on the pinball machine. We got a canoe, not a ski boat, on my 11th birthday. Jimmy Carter was the president back then. He said it wasn't just a recession; it was a malaise. Whatever. I was the king of the lake in my canoe and it's still hanging in my parent's garage if I need it.

===

The "Great Recession" of 2009 actually hit

Northwest Ohio in 2008 when the Big Three automakers failed to make a profit for the first time since 1954. The unemployment rate in Williams County was the highest in the nation for most of that year. I missed all of that and the "pain at the pump" when gas sold at $4 per gallon but when I got home from Iraq everybody looked like they had just been through a mortar attack. People are a lot like deer in that nothing in our history has ever prepared us for loud explosions. When the Big Giant Voice on Joint Base Balad announced "Incoming!" everybody ran to a bunker and waited for the shelling to stop. If a round hit before the warning came they'd just stand around and stare at the crater. You think it would be the opposite way but it never was.

Massive unemployment destroyed the local tax base so fast and hard that Williams County commissioners Brian Davis, Lew Hilkert and Al Word (the retired sheriff) held an emergency meeting that February

"All sources of revenue for the county – from sales taxes to interest from investments – are down because of the economic hit Ohio has taken," Davis said. They called for an immediate 13 percent budget reduction across the board.

For Sheriff Kevin Beck, that was a $194,000 cut from his $1.49 million budget.

Seventy percent of his budget ($1.04 million) was dedicated to wages for union employees under negotiated contracts so he proposed concessions – reducing work weeks from 40 to 32 hours, cutting holiday overtime and educational benefits, and repeating a three-percent pay raise and future stepped salary increases. The union met and deadlocked over whether or not to accept them. The tie vote made Beck personally responsible for his own budget cuts and on April 1, 2009, April Fools Day, he laid off seven of his 18 deputies and one administrative staffer.

Kevin Beck

"Delivering the eight layoff notices was very similar to delivering a death notice," Beck said at the time.

Forty percent of the county's police force disappeared overnight and Beck reorganized his entire staff. Two detectives, three supervisors and one undercover narcotics agent lost their positions and got thrown back on the road patrol. When the Skelton brothers disappeared on Nov. 26, 2010, the Williams County Sheriff's Office was still at odds with itself. The union cast an historic "no confidence" vote against Beck before the end of the year and he resigned before the end of his term.

Beck was a good sheriff and a great guy. We still go to the same church and I see him with his family every Sunday but we haven't spoken since he left office.

===

Janes Snively

James Snively was Beck's chief deputy and he was more than happy to talk when I called him in 2016.

"The old Kunkle school was the first place we checked," he said, because during his first interrogation Skelton said he had a dream about seeing the brothers there.

"The FBI went out there and had words with Sheriff Beck," Snively said. "It was private property and (Beck) said that even if they were the FBI they couldn't just go trampling through without permission. It wasn't a bad conversation, not heated or anything, it's just that the sheriff would have been the guy to catch flak over it if they did.

"We checked ... My gosh we checked everything," Snively said. "Roads, ditches, ponds, abandoned houses, barns and campgrounds. One of the deputies had to search the county landfill with the FBI. That was a miserable job. Glad I didn't get it.

"We checked dumpsters and anything else you could hide stuff in," Snively said. "The search was extensive but nothing ever came of it. Very frustrating. I saw more abandoned buildings and basements than I ever wanted to see.

"Everyone was involved one way or another," Snivley said. "Every call we sent somebody out and documented it to a T. We didn't turn over a tire without writing it down in case something came up down the line. Kevin and I went out when we had to. We talked to Weeks in Morenci on a daily basis and asked what he wanted us to do with the tips. You know how tips are. Every one of them has to be vetted and verified."

One tip even came from his own sister-in-law.

"I was with family at Thanksgiving dinner and she said she'd passed by the Lazy River Campground on her way to Michigan and saw a light on," Snively said. "She thought that was strange for that time of year.

"I wish (Skelton) would just talk and get it over with," Snivley said. "I talked to somebody about it just the other day and they thought he did it just to keep the kids from his crazy wife, but here's the deal – I don't think she's crazy. I saw how she acted, how she talked. With crazy people, you just know. They do or say something and you know they're a bit off. She was never like that."

I asked Snively what he thought happened and where the kids are now.

"I think they're gone and their father did it," he said. "I find it odd that he came to Williams County, especially that time of night. It was a holiday and everything was closed. That means he probably left them here but nobody knows where. Why else would he come here?

"I asked myself a lot when I was in the department, why do people come here to cause trouble?" he said. "Did they just pick us out on a map? I mean, there's the Turnpike but that runs east across the state and out west across several more. Why stop here?

"I still pray they are found but I hope it's not here because that means we failed," he said. "The report has never been closed and it still bugs me. Of all the cases I've done, some still do. It's personal ... But yeah, I think they're here too, unfortunately.

"Eighty percent sure," he said.

I asked him about the layoffs in 2009 and whether they had an impact on the search for the brothers and he said no. "There were so many organizations and agencies, so many volunteers involved it more than well made up for any lack of manpower in our office."

===

A Boy Scout, by definition, is trustworthy, loyal, helpful, friendly, courteous, kind, obedient, cheerful, thrifty, brave, clean and reverent but I was not. I ripped the wings off of flies when I was eight, sipped a beer at my uncle's house when I was ten and smoked a cigarette behind a bowling alley when I was 12. I played poker for pretzels on camping trips and won more than I lost, though not by much. I took a yard chair to Boy Scout Camp Lakota in Defiance one summer and wouldn't let anybody else sit in it.

Jim Snively has never done anything like that. He's been arrow-straight his whole life and he's an Eagle Scout like astronaut Neil Armstrong. He never brags about that because Eagle Scouts never do but you always know they are because they sweat that stuff out their pores. If Neil hadn't flown to the moon in 1969 I would have taken my kids to the James Q. Snively Museum in Wapakonata last summer. I have no idea what Jim's middle name is but I hope it's Quigly because "Quigly Down Under" is still one of my favorite movies and Tom Selleck just gets better with age. I always wanted to grow a mustache and mooch off rich people in Hawaii like Magnum P.I. but Tom Selleck is a skin-lipped New York City police commissioner focused on ethics in "Blue Bloods" now and that's the kind of guy James Snively has always been so disagreeing with him isn't something I take lightly.

I covered the search in 2010, watched it come together and followed the teams wherever they went. Weeks ran the criminal investigation from his office in Morenci and Schissler coordinated the search parties from his office next door. Neither one of them knew the terrain in Williams County as well as the deputies who patrolled it every day. Almost half of those deputies were gone before the search ever started and the rest had been effectively demoted. They didn't plan or execute the search, they supported it.

===

Snively ran against Steve Towns for the sheriff's candidacy in the 2012 Republican primary and lost. Towns won the general election by a landslide and took office in 2013. He didn't fire Snively. He eliminated the whole chief deputy job position. (We still don't have one as of 2018 "because I just don't see the need for it," Towns said.)

Right after Towns took office we did our first interview. I hadn't earned the right to go back to his office yet so we did it in the interrogation room. The missing brothers case was still a sore spot in the community so I pressed it hard and interrogated him until he opened "The Skelton File."

It was less than 12 pages.

"It's just reports about deputies escorting the search teams," he said. "That's about it."

I don't doubt Jim's word. He and Beck did everything he said and probably a lot more and those reports went straight to Weeks in Morenci because he was the lead investigator. All of those reports together stacked up five feet high, table to ceiling, Weeks said when I talked to him in 2012.

The problem was not that the Williams County Sheriff's Office didn't do enough; they did too much. Everybody was on the road tracking down leads or providing security for search teams and nobody was sitting down behind a desk.

For nine days in 2010 Morenci Police Chief Larry Weeks had the best staff in the nation. State police came in from multiple states. The FBI sent profilers, investigators and interrogators. The Center for Missing and Exploited Children sent in Team Adam, the best of all those guys retired from the last generation to advise and assist the next. But staff is a team sport and the one guy Weeks did not have was a mid-level detective who grew up working the Williams County beat.

If that guy had been in Weeks' conference room

working plans with the rest of his staff Snively would not have asked about what to do with tips. That guy would have already laid out what to look for and how to report it and he would have been the one to take the calls.

That guy would have stood up after the FBI agent offered to water board John Skelton and said something like "Don't bother. We have this old disciplinary chair from the jail. Just send him down and strap him in until he wets himself. It's a lot less paperwork."

If that guy had been in the conference room 16 hours a day while the experts debated the meanings of their findings and briefed their reports in front of the map he would've pointed a finger and said "Everything you're talking about comes together right there."

I know this because when I asked Weeks about Williams County Road O.30 he said "I never knew it existed." It wasn't on the map his staff was using because it doesn't exist anymore, not officially. The road was vacated in 1956 because of flooding but part of it is still out there. It runs along the east bank of the St. Joseph River, across from the Lazy River Campground, for about three-quarters of a mile from U.S. 20A. It's easy to miss. I parked my truck on in it when I interviewed divers on Dec. 2, 2010, and never knew it was there.

Chapter 7
The Road That Matters

John Skelton isn't the first guy to be accused of killing his kids. The official name for it, according to Wikipedia, is filicide and Dr. Philip J. Resnick did a study on it in 1969 called "Child Murder by Parents: A Psychiatric Review of Filicide." Resnick said there were five common motives that drove parental child killers.

Altruistic filicide is based on the belief that the parent is "relieving the child of real or imagined suffering."

Spousal revenge filicide includes children killed "to retaliate against or punish the parent's mate."

Acute psychosis filicide includes murder "under the influence of severe mental illness."

Unwanted-child filicide is usually committed by mothers involving newborns.

Accidental filicide results from domestic violence or child abuse.

Skelton claimed altruistic motives. He initially told police his wife was a registered sex offender and he took the kids away to keep them safe, but transcripts from his sentencing hearing in June 2011 indicate revenge and retaliation. Under questioning he said things like "They're going to hibernate until they graduate" and "They won't be coming back until Tanya and I get back together."

Transcripts also show that he turned over the kids' tooth brushes and winter coats to a relative with instructions they don't give them back to his wife because he "didn't want her to have any memories of them." His goal wasn't amnesia. It was more like "You can't even think about the kids without coming back to me."

Zuvers said he acted out of fear because he lost his daughter in a custody battle with his first wife and they live in Massachusetts so he rarely sees her. "I think that was the biggest thing he was afraid of, that he was going to lose his sons," she said. *(Crime Watch Daily, 2015)*

If that is the case and all Skelton wanted was possession of his sons he should be dead. Somebody should have found his body lying next to the kids with a five-page melodramatic suicide note explaining how everyone drove him to drastic action – his wife, his ex-wife, the cops, the judge, the bosses who fired him, the grocery store bagger who put a gallon of milk on top of his eggs so they couldn't make French toast Friday morning. Everybody's to blame, damn it, but we're at peace now because we're going to be together forever.

But that didn't happen.

If police are right, John Skelton killed the three kids in his house, left and came back, then left again, so what else did he want?

Skelton did one phone interview after he was sentenced, on June 29, 2011, with WXYZ out of Detroit. *(WXYZ, 2011)*

He said he pled no contest to unlawful imprisonment because it was his "only chance of getting out.

"The bad thing about innocent until proven

guilty and my Fifth Amendment rights, ya know, it doesn't cover what people think," he said.

If he hadn't been charged with a crime and incarcerated "the kids could be back here in, within three months from now ... But they don't believe me. So it's their loss. It's Tanya's loss and it's my loss and it's my parents' loss and it's her parents' loss. Everybody loses because nobody cares and everybody wants to believe Tanya."

Then he said "If I could keep this, just keep Tanya out of it, then the boys would come back. But I can't so everyone has to stay out of it."

He also said "I know I'll be charged with murder" so why doesn't he just come clean and start building his defense around an insanity plea? He's lodged himself right in the middle of this thing and taken the one course of action that makes it impossible for anyone else to find the kids. That's probably the whole point. He wants to make it hard. He's the only person who knows what happened and why and where, and silence is victory when nobody knows what you're trying to win.

Skelton's last chance to seize that kind of control was the Thanksgiving weekend before the divorce was final but the one thing that could bring it all crashing down was outside interference, like when police intervened during the trip to Florida with Andrew and Alexander in September, 2010. That was the biggest risk he wanted to avoid and it still is.

Police assumed, at least publicly, that Skelton "disposed of" the bodies, dumping them somewhere without telling anybody. Everyone involved in the search brought their A-game and set out to do the most good in the fastest time but if Skelton wanted (and still wants) to exercise the most control as long as possible, "Where are they?" is the wrong question. It's a dead end that defines the search as a process of elimination. Weeks himself said most of his reports were sworn statements saying "Nope. Not here. Not there." If Skelton wants to stay in control, simply disposing the bodies doesn't work. He had to intentionally conceal them so no one could find them without knowing where to look. The better question would have been "Where can this guy hide three bodies?"

I figured all that out all by myself in a day and felt pretty good about it until I called Harness again.

He said "Yeah dude, that's his Happy Place ... What do we know about it?"

"Uh, it wasn't happy?"

"No dude.Think," he said. "What can you tell me ABOUT it?"

It was almost midnight when I called and I could tell his patience was limited. I started flipping notebook pages close the phone so he could hear them. It's a great trick I learned dealing with angry customers. It makes me sound busy and buys time.

"Cops pinged his phone off the cell tower in Holiday City so it's probably close," I blurted out.

"Probably is good enough if that's all you got," Harness said. "How close?"

"Seven mile circle," I said. "We had 16 cell towers in a grid; four wide-four deep. Holiday City was inside the grid and his phone never touched the edges."

He asked what all that meant and I explained that Skelton most likely drove into Williams County from Morenci without stopping, spent time here and went back home. The Holiday City cell phone tower was the center of his circle so he probably spent 76 minutes within three-and-a-half miles of it. Police never got a report of where the cell phone pings piled up and nobody ever tracked the trail of pings along the roadways that should have led to the piles.

"So what can this guy do in 76 minutes?" Harness asked.

"My cops think he sunk them, probably off a bridge, but I don't," I said. "Seventy-six minutes is too long for that. And a guy on a bridge looks like a jumper. He wouldn't want that." (Our best known urban legend involves an old bridge in the Lost Nation State Game Area, 14 miles north of the Michigan state line. After the Civil War, a lady supposedly jumped off with her baby and still haunts it. Everybody knows somebody who's gone up there and heard the screams. Whether it's true or not doesn't really matter. Anybody standing on a bridge at night around here is going to get somebody's attention.)

"And he wants to bring them back," I said. "Says they're supposed to hibernate 'til they graduate. A river would take them away."

"So what can he do in 76 minutes?" Harness asked again.

"Hide them in a woods," I said, "but 76 minutes

isn't long enough. Not to carry bodies through brush three times in the dark. And he wasn't scratched up and his minivan wasn't dirty."

"So what's that tell you?" Harness asked. "Easy in and easy out? Close to a road?"

"Probably."

===

I started driving around Holiday City in my spare time, of which there wasn't much, so it was a lot of short trips spread over a couple weeks. I was looking for places close to the road where a guy could park for an hour without being noticed while he carried three bodies in and out and not trip over stuff.

I found five:

Oliver's Bridge is about two miles west-northwest of Holiday City, on County Road N between the Ohio Turnpike and the Lazy River Campground. The woods come right up to the road on both sides so it would be easy to park and spend time there. I know that place was searched in 2010 because I saw teams in the woods. Snively was out there too and he wasn't having a good day. He was cold and wet when I drove by and I've never seen him looking more frustrated. I ruled it out.

I found a large culvert a mile east of Holiday City where the Norfolk Southern railroad tracks make a triangle with County Road N.30 and County Road 16. It had a five-foot diameter so you walk through it stooped. I ruled that out because a rock-lined erosion ditch stretches past farm houses within a quarter mile on both sides of the road. Even if Skelton slipped in and out that Friday morning the bodies would have been noticeable a short time later.

I found a medium-sized culvert a mile west of Kunkle, on County Road O at County Road 16. It's big enough to crawl through and it was half-filled with silt. There's even a tractor trail within 50 yards of it. Kunkle has a cell phone tower but if Skelton had parked facing west and left his phone in the Dodge Caravan (which he would do if he was planning to crawl through a culvert) the wires in his rear window defroster could have disrupted the signal.

I had a plan to crawl through it myself. I was going to rent a wet suit and probe the silt with a stick. I recruited my photographer to help out. She was going to stand by the road with her press pass and camera so if anybody called the Sheriff's Office she could explain who we were. If I found anything, she was going to call for a fire department's hazardous materials team to scrub me down. She offered to tie a rope to my ankles and pull me out with her Ford Escort if I got stuck.

But then County Engineer Todd Roth caught on to my sudden interest in his drainage program and called the paper. He wanted to know what I was looking for and I said "It's actually a story that has nothing to do with you." Todd's a great guy and he's been a friend of my father-in-law since before I was married. I could have told him everything but I was on deadline right then and I'm kind of a jerk when it comes to elected officials – if they don't have to tell me what's going on in their executive sessions, I don't have to tell them what I'm working on.

Todd called back a couple hours later and said he "just happened to be looking through his records" and realized that particular culvert hadn't been cleaned out in quite a while so he was sending a crew out next week to take care of it. They didn't find anything.

===

The biggest culvert I found was on U.S. 20A two miles north of Holiday City, between the Lazy River Campground and Ohio 15. There's an abandoned RV dealership on the south side of the road and he could have parked there. The area is wide open. The erosion ditch is huge, about 20 feet wide, and easily seen from the road. U.S. 20A is one of the busiest roads in the county so somebody would have seen something by now.

Skelton told police he had wrapped the kids in blankets and gave each of the kids a stuffed animal before he left. That part of his story has never changed and seems to be true.

There was a rumor that one of the first search teams found a stuffed animal in a ditch near a gated tractor trail about a half mile west of the culvert so I checked it out.

The gate was open and I drove in because I knew where to park. I walked that trail on Dec. 2, 2010, when I followed the Steuben County Fire Department's dive team. They put in on the north side of the road and floated downstream under the bridge with their sonar. I needed photos so I darted across the road and through the gate, and followed the trail into the woods back to the river. I crawled over a guardrail and crossed another street just as Dennis Wisniewski said "We can see where the deer crossed!" Sonar was picking up tracks in the mud underwater. (He was so impressed by that he told Sheriff Kevin Beck. That's when Beck decided to get a sonar for his own dive team.)

I drove my truck around the guardrail, parked on the asphalt and got out to look around. I didn't really expect to find anything, but you never know. None of the search teams ever went back into the woods because it's all privately owned. I walked along the dirt trail again and paid attention to the ground looking for stuff in the underbrush. Right when I turned around I realized my truck was parked on a street in the middle of a woods. It's an old street with lots of potholes and I followed it through the tunnel of trees. No houses, no fire hydrants, no power lines and no reason at all to be there.

I flew back to the office and told my boss' boss, Times Senior Editor Don Allison, what I found.

He was like "Yeah, that's County Road O.30. I remember passing by there when I was a kid."

I ran down the block to the Local History Center at the Williams County Public Library and found an old county map from 1953. It was there!

I called Roth at the engineer's office and found out the road was abandoned in 1956 because of flood damage. The right-of-way was vacated and absorbed into the adjacent land parcels but the pavement is still there.

It's 2.4 miles north of Holiday City

Chapter 8
The 2013 Search

Al Word was just another politician when I met him in November 2008. He had just taken office as a Williams County commissioner and I was a brand new reporter at The Bryan Times. I got stuck with the local government beat and covered commissioner meetings at the courthouse Mondays and Thursdays because nobody else wanted to.

On Sept. 13, 2010, the commissioners held a town hall meeting at the Williams County Fair. It was a Monday morning and I didn't want to be there. My sister died a week earlier and it was my first day back at work. I wanted to sit in the back of the room and take notes and be ignored but people kept coming up to shake my hand and offer condolences. That's what people do and I appreciate it. I do the same thing but it's always awkward.

After the meeting I walked up to ask questions and found out Word was just as uncomfortable as I was. His father died the same day as my sister and we had a line of people between us shaking hands in both directions. When we finally worked through the crowd he said "Sorry to hear about your sister" and I said "Sorry to hear about your dad."

Then he winked and said "I'm sorrier."

"Yes, but I'm very sorry," I said. He upped the ante and we ran through very, very, very, very, very sorry before we lost count and started laughing. People stared at us with their mouths open but we've been friends ever since.

Word was the first person I ran to when I found out about County Road O.30.

I didn't know if John Skelton ever drove back there or how he would have found it in the first place and I had no way of finding out, I told him. All I knew was that if you're looking for a place to hide three bodies close to Holiday City no other place was better suited and nobody knows about it. We met in the waiting room on the fourth floor of the courthouse, right next to the employee break room. He talked about the grizzly Kozier homicide and I talked about where to hide bodies and, again, people stared at us with their mouths open.

Word finally nodded and said "Listen, you need to tell Steve Towns ... Today."

When I got back to the paper I called for an appointment and got one for the next morning.

===

Towns himself met me at the door and we walked back to his office, not the interrogation room, and he already had maps spread out over his desk.

I told him about the road and how I found it and why I thought it mattered.

Towns said he also heard about the stuffed animal. He said it was an FBI agent right after the Amber Alert went out, before all the volunteers stepped up. They were walking U.S. 20A at night and using flashlights. He wasn't sure exactly where, but it was near the St. Joe River bridge and

Steve Towns

the rusted out gate.

Towns said he had even been down County Road O.30 before, back when he was a deputy and Word was the sheriff. The area "used to be pretty wild, lots of beer and people having sex all over the place," he said. He went out for a noise complaint once and found a couple having sex. He ended up finding two more couples that night. "I patrolled that road a couple times but nothing ever spilled over."

The meeting lasted about an hour and Towns brought in one of his lieutenants who used to work undercover with the Multi-Area Narcotics Task Force. I didn't know that until I saw him in uniform and that's not the first or last time that's happened.

Back when K2 and Spice were all the rage and kids were getting sick on it, I did an interview with a head shop owner. He was an old hippy who loved to talk. He'd call me brother one minute and threaten to kick my ass the next because he wanted the whole world to know he was "doing the Lord's work through enhanced pharmaceuticals" but he had his lawyer on speed dial and he'd call in a heartbeat if I printed anything he said. One of his regulars walked in and just stood there smiling at me with his arms crossed while I was busy not taking notes for a story I wasn't going to write.

That guy is a police captain in Bryan now.

Another time I picked up a traffic stop report from the Bryan Police Department with a K-9 that found drugs but no arrests were made so I started asking questions. Ten minutes later I got a personal call from the Task Force commander and he told me to be in a church parking lot in 10 minutes. Turns out the driver was a confidential informant and they were about to take down a drug house. When the raid started I ran around with my press pass and camera telling everyone "I was invited" and they were all like "We know." When I told my wife about it that night she asked "How'd they get your cell phone number?"

I still don't know.

===

On May 12, 2013, we searched the woods. I brought a notebook and a camera. Towns brought his lieutenant, a couple deputies and Max, a 6-year-old German shepherd K-9.

Towns walked the east side of the river bank and talked to kayakers. He said it was "just a routine patrol for drug activity," which it probably also was. Max is a drug sniffer and the lieutenant walked the west side of the river and never said a word.

"Let us know if you see anything," Towns told the tourists. He asked them to look for methamphetamine labs made out of plastic bottles with white or grey residue, plastic tubing and weird smells but then he added ropes, cords, wires, string and duct tape into the description.

"If that guy wrapped his kids in blankets he had to secure them somehow," he told me quietly after they paddled away. And if that was the case, he said, "it didn't take him 76 minutes. He used 10 or 15 for whatever ceremony was in his freaky little mind."

If Skelton had just 55 minutes to move three bodies over uneven terrain in the dark he had to stay close to his minivan. I criss-crossed the clearing next to the lane and kept my eyes on my feet.

I found an over-grown trench close to a wood line and called Towns. He didn't answer so I called again.

He came out of the woods about 50 feet away and asked "Why you burning up my phone?"

"Looks like a grave," I said, pointing down at the trench. It was about four feet long and two feet wide and the grass was taller and greener then everything else around it.

Towns said "Nope. We know he didn't bury them. Wasn't dirty enough. Didn't have a shovel. Didn't have any tools. Didn't have enough time."

Deputy Ryan Baird found a couple bones in the bushes close to U.S. 20 and bagged them as evidence but said "Don't get excited. A lot of people have found stuff like this since 2010 and it's usually deer." (A DNA test from the state's Bureau of Criminal Investigation lab in Bowling Green later confirmed they were from a deer, just as he predicted.)

Deputy Scott Shuping and Max walked the

roadway up one side and down the other but never found anything. They had also walked the Holiday City retention pond in 2012 after Surat Nuenoom disappeared. They did three laps, Beck said at the time, and never picked up a scent.

It's not the dog's fault.

In the "Cadaver Dog Handbook: Forensic Training and Tactics for the Recovery of Human Remains," authors Andrew Reman, Edward David and Marcella H. Sorg note that "At the time of biological death, the individual scent emitted by the subject undergoes a transformation" and that change in the scent profile leads to a change in a tracking dog's behavior.

"A phenomenon that has been noted by many tracking/trailing dog handlers is that some dogs will follow a trail, often many days old, but fail to close in on the body if the subject is deceased," the authors noted. "They may register the scent change and, whether from fear, difference in odor, or some other reason, may not approach. If the handler had never observed this behavior before, he or she might assume the dog had lost the scent trail. In reality, the dog is showing aversion to cadaver scent. The dog may show aversion by its hackles raising, circling, or other behavior that indicates that it does not want to approach an area. Through training these behaviors can be overcome." *(Rebmann, 2000)*

Max was a tracking/trailing K-9 with a long history of successful tracks on live suspects and drugs but he was never trained to identify cadaver scent or provide a clear signal if he did.

===

Deputy Rex Lawrence searched the south end of the clearing and found a baseball. He called Towns so we all went over to check it out.

It was down an overgrown trail about 20 yards east of the river bank and perched in the fork of a tree about three feet high.

The ball was clean and white and almost new but the red stitching and blue lettering were faded. It was a 2010 Spaulding Little League T-ball, lot number 15450. Lawrence and Towns put on latex gloves and stuffed it into an orange evidence bag.

Towns said the woods was "hot" and that they should try to find out if Skelton had ever asked anyone for permission to fish back there but he still had a list of other hot areas in the county. He favored Lake Pioneer and the two bridges over the East Branch of the St. Joseph River. One bridge was on U.S. 20 between the lake and Floral Grove Cemetery. Another was on Ohio 15 about two miles south of Pioneer but I disagreed. Pioneer had a cell phone tower in 2010. If he parked there his phone should have hit that one, not Holiday City's.

There is another bridge on U.S. 20 over the West Branch of the St. Joe, about a mile northwest of where we were standing. Towns said that was hot, too. I disagreed, but not as much. Skelton's cell phone could have hit either tower from there, but there are no other roads. Skelton would have had to park his minivan on the highway and in the open for more than an hour. I don't think he would have done that.

===

Towns had the BCI lab results from the baseball when I walked into his office on Sept. 10, 2013. He said they were "inconclusive -- no prints, no DNA."

I asked about going back to the woods and the other areas with cadaver dogs and he said the problem was manpower. Nobody has enough, not to commit resources on a reporter's hunch. "I never had use for Sherlock Holmes stuff," he said. "Give me facts and leads I can track down."

That's when he whipped out the knife hands and said "Look. You know everything we know. There are a couple little details we're never going to tell you and that's just the way it's going to be. We're protecting the integrity of the investigation. They're little things. They're not game changers. You know everything else."

Towns and his deputies have done other searches since then. A tip led them to an abandoned house in June 2015, and they helped the Fulton County Sheriff's Office track down a tip they got that same summer. I didn't find out about either search until they were over and the only statement I got from Towns and Brewer was that "We didn't find anything."

The fact that I got invited to any search at all was a miracle.

I started working on this book in 2015, the same year Rex Lawrence left the road patrol to take over courthouse security. One day I asked him about the search and why they let me go. He said "Al Word called us."

Chapter 9
Hembree's Insight

In all my life I've met just two people named Rex – Rex Lawrence the sheriff's deputy and Rex Ridgway the T-ball coach in West Unity when I was seven. I still get them confused. I interviewed Lawrence about a drug bust once and quoted him as Ridgway. Towns called the next morning and said "What the hell are you doing? Ridgway was Adam's dad. He doesn't know anything about meth!"

Ridgway was a great guy with saintly patience. I never figured out how to hit a ball on a stick with a stick and the one time he made me catcher I got mad at the pitcher and told him to aim for my glove. I spent the rest of the season in right field. I got hit in the face by a bouncing grounder once so I always dodged the ball after that and chased it down after it rolled past. We didn't win a single game but Ridgway bought us all ice cream cones at the end of the season so it was kind of worth it. I still have a Post-it note on my monitor that says "Ridgway is ice cream/Lawrence is handcuffs." It's right next to "Lead is for pencils and led is for people." My editor gave me that one.

===

Inconclusive is a terrible word, like undiagnosed.

It means you could be right about something being wrong but nobody knows which is which.

The fact that we found a 2010 Little League baseball back in the woods where I predicted three kids from 2010 should be may be a total coincidence but I doubted it. It's a rutted up clearing with tall grass surrounded by trees. Nobody would ever play catch back there and if they wanted batting practice we should have found a hundred balls on the ground, not one perched in a tree. Somebody put it there for a reason and I desperately wanted to find out if he was from Morenci. I called three sporting goods stores in Adrian – Dunham's, Johnson's Sporting Goods and Outdoors Again – because they seemed to the best source of baseballs for Morenci. None of them carried Spaulding Little League baseballs. I called Wal-Marts in Adrian, Jonesville and Ann Arbor and they didn't carry them either. An employee of our own sporting goods store here in Bryan, Bill's Locker Room III, said "It just isn't an off-the-shelf item."

I called Spaulding's corporate office in Bowling Green, Kentucky, and talked to Dave Coradini, vice president of sales and sponsorships. I told him I was a reporter and I wanted to know if they had shipped any baseballs from Lot Number 15450 to Morenci in 2010 because one of them may be connected to a disappearance. He transferred me over to his public relations guy Dave Shivel who bounced me over to their attorney while I was still talking. That guy gave me a four-minute lecture and the gist was that if I couldn't prove a Spaulding product was involved in a crime I shouldn't be calling them and if I could prove it they'd never talk to me anyway.

Chayse Held was The Bryan Times sports editor and his desk was right next to mine. When I hung up the phone he said "Spauldings are expensive. Most leagues around here use Diamonds for regular season play because they're cheaper. They save the Spauldings for tournaments."

A hard-to-get tournament ball in the woods at a possible crime scene is every reporter's dream, like knowing why Orson Wells whispered "Rosebud" in Citizen Kane. If any of Skelton's kids played baseball, and if any of the teams in Morenci used Spauldings, it could have been him. If I could prove that, I could break an awesome story.

I found Larry Fix, director of Michigan's Little League District 16 which includes Morenci. He said they did the same thing. "We use Spauldings for tournament play. Regular season (baseballs) are a matter of the best bargain for each team."

He sent me on to Tim Decker, who managed the Little League program in Morenci. He said Andrew and Alexander Skelton may have played a season. If either of them had ever made a great play in a tournament, he couldn't remember.

Nothing made sense because everything almost connected but never did — the baseball shouldn't just be there. Cell phone pings should have told police exactly where Skelton went but they didn't and nobody ever saw what happened. I had nothing else to look for and wasn't even sure what I was looking at.

On a whim, I reached out to Greg Hembree, a

retired military intelligence officer from Indianapolis. We served together in Iraq and I almost saved his life once. I found a land mine at the burn pit on Joint Base Balad right before he drove over it. We called an EOD team and they checked it out. It was a half-buried hubcap from an old Russian truck but it did look like a land mine. I figured Greg kind of owed me a favor. When I told him what I was working on he drove up for a day because he wanted to "see the terrain."

Cops and soldiers both carry guns but they're completely different animals, he said when he got here. "A criminalist, whether a crime scene investigator or a detective, tends to be concerned about finding evidence to support a conviction. They are part of an organization and effort to convict a suspect and put them in jail. Intelligence analysts are focused on everything – all evidence – in order to identify patterns and trends. They want to discover what the reality is. The analyst knows that factors are hidden and understands he needs collectors to bring in a constant stream of data so he can develop the truth of the situation. The analyst realizes that his Monday morning assessment can change dramatically by Wednesday afternoon because the information changes. That drives a whole new analysis and he has to revise his assessment. If a criminalist can't gather enough evidence to convict a suspect, his prosecutor finds other charges to use. There are no suspects or convictions to make in combat. All we have is simple, accurate and true depiction of the battlefield so commanders can close with and destroy an enemy. I've given that lesson to my junior analysts several times, many of which are police officers in their civilian jobs, or they believe that they are some kind of Fox Mulder out to discover some hidden conspiracy."

Closing with John Skelton was impossible. I wrote to him once I found we had something in common and offered to tell his side of the story but he never responded.

Chapter 10

Betrayed by Joanne Taylor

Hembree and I drove through Morenci first, passed Skelton's house at 100 E. Congress St. and Zuvers' house, then we stopped at Riverside Park on the north edge of town, next to Bean Creek.

I told Hembree about the interview with John Walsh and the FBI agent who offered to water board John Skelton. He laughed.

"Skelton wouldn't talk, even if you water boarded him," Hembree said. "Torture doesn't break anybody down. What gets to them is the not knowing. You inflict a little bit of pain so they stress out over the amount of pain they think you're capable of. That's what gets to them ... He won't talk because whatever he wants matters more than whatever he fears."

Then Hembree said "John Skelton doesn't even have to be in jail."

Skelton and Zuvers lived just four blocks apart in a very small town, Hembree said. Morenci has two stop lights and about 2,000 people so everybody pretty much knows everybody else. All he had to say was something like 'Yeah, I had few beers that night and the kids were getting on my nerves so I sent 'em home. I even gave them my cell phone and told them to call if they got scared in the dark.'

"He wouldn't have won Father of the Year with that story, but when police started asking questions about what happened to the kids, all his bases would have been covered," Hembree said. "When they started searching for the kids, he could have been right there in it helping them out. He could have been leading them this way or that to suit his purposes.

"The point," Hembree said, "is that he could have built a simple, unbeatable alibi if he wanted to. He could have even implicated his wife like 'What!? They never made it? They never called so I assumed everything was ... My God, what has she done!?'

"He had a good plan, but only up to a point," Hembree said. "Joann Taylor was a stupid mistake. He didn't need her and he shouldn't have gone there. That's what put him in jail."

The problem for Skelton was that something went wrong, Hembree said. I asked what that could be and he just stared me.

"Nobody ever plans to break an ankle," he said.

Chapter 11
Suicide Story

"If John Skelton met up with a secret organization in a parking lot early that morning and turned over the kids like he said, his ankle never would have been broken," Hembree said. "What could have caused it there?

"My bet is he broke it while he was getting rid of the bodies," he said. "Rough terrain in the dark. Stressed out more than he's ever been before. His center of gravity's off because his carrying an extra 50 pounds. Trips over a log or steps in a hole. That's all it would take. When he gets back home and the adrenaline wears off he's like 'Oh man, this shit really hurts!'

"The truth is he had a really good plan," Hembree said. "He controlled all of the variables he planned for but then lost control of the ones he didn't."

There was no Joanne Taylor and John Skelton never wanted to die, he said.

===

Skelton was in a Toledo hospital when Weeks caught up with him that Friday.

His story was that he called Taylor to pick up the kids and take them down to his parent's house in Florida because he was going to kill himself, but then he broke his ankle during the suicide attempt.

That's when he called another friend for a ride to the hospital, the one in Toledo 38 miles east and on the other side of the state line, not the one four blocks away on the west side of Morenci.

On Dec. 1, 2010, five days after the kids were reported missing, Skelton's sister Lucinda Ford did a phone interview with The Detroit Free Press from her home in Jacksonville, Florida. She said she spoke to Skelton twice after his alleged suicide attempt, once before he got arrested and once after. (Detroit Free Press, 2015) He told her he was depressed because he had lost his job for "taking time off work to see his sons when their mother wouldn't allow it."

She said her brother wanted to kill himself that morning but then he changed his mind at the last second. He was going to hang himself "from a banister leading down into the basement" but then "When he tried to get down, he lost his footing and fell to the concrete floor," she said. That's when he "broke his ankle and lost consciousness."

Skelton's father, William, didn't buy the suicide story at all. He and his wife, Roxanne, met with Skelton at the Lucas County Jail on Dec. 9, 2010, and spoke to reporters outside afterward.

When a reporter from WTOL-TV in Toledo asked "Do you think (your son) is suicidal?" William said no "Because he's got more character than that. I don't think he's ever been really, honestly suicidal. Attention getting? To get stuff going? Yeah, I wouldn't doubt that from my son. I wouldn't doubt that a bit." *(WTOL, 2010)*

Then the reporter asked "Do you think he did try to hang himself?" and again William said no. "He was a Boy Scout. I know how his knot tying capability is. I know what his mechanical capabilities are. If he wanted to kill himself by hanging himself he could have done that easy enough without muffing it."

The suicide attempt was just "attention getting," he said again.

===

Skelton was arrested as soon as he was released from the hospital on Dec. 2, 2010, and had to appear in the Lucas County Court of Common Pleas for an extradition hearing. He was in a wheelchair but he was wearing a soft shoe cast.

If he fell like he said, he should have been wearing a hard plaster cast, according to Dr. Charles Felix, emergency department director at Community Hospitals and Wellness Centers-Bryan. The soft shoe cast indicated a hairline fracture, a cracked bone, not a full break.

"When you fall from a height of 10 feet you will not get a hairline fracture of the ankle," Felix said in 2017. "Usually it is a displaced fracture (when a bone snaps into two pieces and the ends no longer line up like they should). Also, a fall from that type of height will involve the lumbar spine."

There should have been compression fractures along the vertebrae, he said, and that should have kept Skelton down in a hospital bed a lot longer than he was.

Dr. John Moats, who served as the coroner of Williams County for 30 years, from 1974 to 2004, agreed with Felix's assessment but added questions of his own. "Yes," he said. "I would expect more severe injuries in a direct 10-foot fall onto a concrete floor. However, I would like to see the design of the staircase. Was there railing on the staircase? Could he have been on one of the lower steps or the landing prior to the fall? Were any of the staircase railings broken? Of course, it would be important to know how he fell, i.e. headfirst, sideways or other position to determine what his injuries might have been. Was the rope recovered? If so, was it loose or tied around the railing or other object and where was it located? I would have to say I would not consider myself an expert on falls such as this. I would be looking for further information if available."

When I asked Felix how hairline fractures happen, he said they "usually indicated twisting or rolling. He might have inflicted this injury while walking in uneven terrain."

Whatever actually happened that Friday morning, evidence indicates it didn't happen the way John Skelton said.

Chapter 12

Shoulda Known Better

I'm very aware of the fact that it's more fun being me than it is putting up with people like me. That's why I never tried to talk to Tanya Zuvers. Every time I saw her she was surrounded by television crews with lights, cameras and one of those giant Q-Tip microphones so I always made it a point to leave her alone. When we crossed paths on the Heartland set in Perrysburg I smiled and got out of the room as fast as I could. (And my photographer left her purse in my truck. Her boyfriend picked her up while I was still doing the interview and she was burning up my phone to get it back. Face time with John Walsh is a once-in-a-lifetime event so I let ring. Let me say, one more time, how very sorry I am.)

In 2010, a newspaper in Detroit reported that John Skelton had served in the Air Force but that never made sense to me. The "Missing in Morenci" Facebook page had a photo of all three brothers wearing gray Army physical fitness T-shirts. March 8, 2016, was a slow news day so I shot a message to the page administrator. In all honesty, I was just trying to look productive and never expected a response.

I told them I was a reporter and wrote "Vets from one branch of military service typically don't get stuff for their kids from the other branches. Do you happen to know if John Skelton actually served in the Army? Do you know what his job in the military was?"

Zuvers herself responded that Skelton had actually served in the Army.

He was a medic, like me, about the same time I was. I did one tour with an ambulance company in Korea (where I found out my battalion commander was from Bryan and related to my dad's insurance agent so I celebrated Christmas with his family in Seoul). My second tour was with a light infantry brigade at Fort Lewis in Washington state. Skelton did his tours as a hospital medic – Walter Reed National Military Medical Center in Washington D.C., Tripler Army Medical Center in Hawaii and Bassett Army Community Hospital in Anchorage, Alaska.

That was where he met his first wife, Zuvers said. She was the one in the Air Force. She had more rank and better pay so Skelton left the Army to follow her career. He moved back to Morenci with their daughter after the couple separated in 2000, and that first divorce led to his second from Zuvers.

He and Zuvers met through a mutual friend. "It was still early in our relationship and he was still hoping to get back together with his wife," Zuvers said. "Then one day I get this phone call from the school.

"We found out his wife was there," Zuvers said. "She drove all the way from Boston to the Toledo Airport and rented a car. Then she came to Morenci, walked right into school through the north door, didn't stop at the office or anything, and tried to take their daughter out of class. They've been locking that door ever since. We found out she had all the paperwork to get custody back in Massachusetts stashed in her own car. He fought it and lost and she went to Boston anyway.

"He said he lost his daughter because of me, because of my criminal history," Zuvers said. "I used to believe that."

When Skelton and Zuvers separated in September 2010, he followed the same plan and pulled Andrew and Alexander out of school. They called the police because it was only the second week of class and there was no reason for him to ask for their birth certificates, she said. No charges were ever filed but she got full custody of the boys because of it.

"I met his first wife once. We talked and got along fine," Zuvers said. "When my boys disappeared she said she wanted nothing to do with it and asked not to be contacted."

No one ever has.

===

Skelton and Zuvers couldn't get along under the same roof but they still did family stuff together that summer, before he pulled the kids out of school.

"We just started getting into tent camping and went twice," Zuvers said.

Their first trip was a big family gathering on Memorial Day weekend at Loveberry's Funny

Farm, 8.1 miles north of Holiday City.

In August, they took a second trip to Harrison Lake State Park, 10 miles east of Holiday City.

"The kids had a four-day weekend and wanted to get away because there was a lot of tension," Zuvers said. "We weren't living in the same house anymore." She and the boys stayed in her parent's camper. She took a lot of pictures and most of them are hanging on the wall in her living room.

"We had two tragedies that fall," Zuvers said. "One of the high school kids went out rabbit hunting and never came home. Never even made it out to the woods. His feet got tangled in some vines. He tripped and his gun went off. He was only 14. Five weeks later my boys disappeared. It was rough on the whole town."

===

Yellow ribbons started popping up in Morenci during the search but the media wasn't kind after news of Zuvers' 1998 misdemeanor sexual conduct conviction broke.

A Detroit TV station "reported we were having parties and that's not true," she said. "My whole family came in and we stayed at my parent's house. Everybody made food and we ate in the garage. They were filming inside, through windows on the deck, and we had to tape newspapers over them."

The house was crowded with one bathroom so a

neighbor paid to have a Port-A-John set in the backyard. Inside the house there were lines even family could not cross. Everybody stayed in the garage and the living room at one end while Zuvers retreated to a bedroom in the other. "One of my sisters posted herself as a guard and nobody ever got through that door," she said.

A local business donated milk for all the kids in the family. "There was an FBI Agent named Scott and he came over every day, sometimes a couple times a day," she said. "My niece had a crush on him. When she found out he liked chocolate milk she'd run out and get him two cartons every time."

The search ended on Friday, Dec. 3, 2010, but when Agent Scott stopped by the day before he told Zuvers and her family about the massive search on the Lazy River Campground 3.7 miles north of Holiday City.

"I had no idea why," Zuvers said. "We never camped there. He was a truck driver for a company in Goshen, Indiana, and he had a milk route on U.S. 20. He drove by the place a gazillion times.

"I thought they were tracking his cell phone," she said. "He had promised to pay for a family plan after the divorce started but he didn't. He said he couldn't afford it so his mommy got him a new one."

Chapter 13

Brock on the River

When I took Greg Hembree out to Williams County Road O.30, he said the baseball we found made sense but it probably wasn't as significant as I thought.

"He'd want to keep the kids close together," Hembree said. "If he wanted to 'bring them back' when his wife came back that's the most sensible plan. But it's easy to get lost in the woods, in the dark.

"That ball was probably just a trail marker," he said. "He walked along the wood line and followed the trail deeper in but he needs the ball to make sure he can find the same trail three times over. It's just a practical thing that he forgets about it when he's done. He'd be tired after the effort, exhausted and stressed out."

"So if the ball was here and the bodies weren't, where are they?" I asked.

"Don't know," he said. "Does the river flood?"

===

I called the National Weather Service Office in North Webster, Indiana, to request flood data on the St. Joseph River and found out the Village of Montpelier had a weather station at their wastewater plant on the St. Joe 6.5 miles downstream from the woods.

The average slope of the St. Joe River bottom is 1.6 feet per mile so the water flows slow and brown, not fast and white. Flood stage starts when the river crests at 12 feet and there was no flooding reported in 2010. In 2011, the river crested at 12.55 feet on March 7; 12.09 feet on March 30; 13.52 feet on May 28 and 12.37 feet on Nov. 25. It crested at 15.51 feet on Dec. 1, the eighth highest level on record from the village. It also crested at 12.33 feet on Dec. 7 and 12.67 feet on Dec. 18.

The weather station shut down at the end of 2011 due to lack of funding and the daily records stopped. The report said 2012 was a drought year, "likely no flooding between March and December." There was no data at all for 2013.

===

I spoke to Doug Rowland, who owns the Lazy River Campground, after Hembree's tour in 2015. If anybody ever found anything, it would have been him.

"To be honest, when we cleaned it up last summer we found very little trash in the river, which is a good sign," Rowland said. "There were pretty good log jams out there, all kinds of leaves and limbs but very little trash which is a great thing."

He also said he wasn't the only person who worked on the river.

Brock McClanahan owned and operated B Rocks Canoe and Kayak Livery on the St. Joe from 2012 to 2017. Managing a fleet of boats and keeping customers happy was easy but keeping the river clear was not. "That was a full-time job," he said. "We cleared log jams in the river from Pioneer (4.8 miles north of Holiday City) to Oliver's Bridge (about a hundred yards north of the Ohio Turnpike). They were about 50 feet apart at first and you could tell it had been neglected for a long time.

"We picked up about 20 truckloads of trash every spring," McClanahan said. "Standard trash; TVs, tires, lots of random stuff. A lot of kids' shoes. Everything people throw into ditches gets washed into the river. Big storms always wash in a lot of debris. We'd clear stuff one day and go back the next after a big storm. It was like we were never there.

"There's a marsh (between the Lazy River Campground and Oliver's Bridge) and it floods a lot," McClanahan said. "After the kids disappeared, a friend of their family came and asked if I could take them down the river. They said they had a weird, creepy feeling about it but that never happened. I didn't have approval to go anywhere off river and they lost interest.

"That marsh can be tricky," McClanahan said. "It floods a lot and everything comes in. Lots of silt and bean stubble from the fields. If they were back there it wouldn't take much to cover them."

From Oliver's bridge to Montpelier, the river is still blocked, McClanahan said. "Log jams every hundred yards or so. A demolition crew contracted with the watershed commission but they don't do much.

"I know the river better than anybody," McClanahan said. "If they were within 50 feet of it, they never came up."

Chapter 14

Walk in the Woods

John Skelton is still winning because he owns the facts about what he did and where he went but information always leaves a pattern. My theory is that if you can see the pattern, find the gaps and fill them in you can search what's left. In 2010 the search area for three boys included everywhere their father could have taken them – 80 square miles across three counties in three states covering 51,200 acres with more than 500 volunteers. My final gap is only 197 acres in the low ground between the Lazy River Campground and the Ohio Turnpike along Williams County Road O.30. That's less than two grid squares on a Universal Transverse Mercator (UTM) map like the Army uses and the Yankee North Land Navigation range at Fort Benning is a whole lot bigger than that. I ran the course 17 times when I was a second lieutenant at the Infantry Officer Basic Course and probably still hold the base record for the most consecutive failures.

It was a heart problem, not a head problem.

I enlisted in 1994 as a private and land navigation was the best part of basic training because the drill sergeants left us alone for five whole hours. It was even more fun when I was an NCO because the privates left me alone for six.

Officer basic is a "gentleman's course" where you go to class and do homework and take tests just like college with a couple weeks in the field. If you don't cheat, get hurt or quit, you pass. It was easy until the day we ate lunch with a full-bird colonel. It was an open forum where anybody could ask questions but he did most of the talking. His speech was all about what he called "living well." Don't drink and drive. Don't drink alone and don't be a jerk when you get drunk. He wasn't too fond of strip clubs either. If you're lucky, you'll get your ass kicked the first time out and never go back. The unlucky ones go back, have sex and get diseases but the truly unfortunate souls fall in love. They live in hell and die broke. The best way to avoid all that was to "Marry above your station," he said. "Find a woman better than you and live up to her expectations."

I wrote a letter to my girlfriend that night and proposed through the mail because it was less frightening than a phone call. A week later she wrote back and turned me down. I always got lost after that. My pace count was 67 steps but I couldn't concentrate past 20. That four months is still a blur. I ate Ranger Burgers and made fun of the overweight Elvis impersonator on the Ezell's Catfish Cabin commercials but everything else was just mud, sweat, kudzu vines and leprous armadillos charging out of the bushes like bowling balls with claws. I got recycled on the morning of graduation day and started the whole thing over that afternoon with Mel Gibson and Sam Elliott. They were on post filming "We Were Soldiers." The production company wanted extras to work the weekends and I could have been Soldier: row three, column four during Gibson's big stadium speech, where says he says "I will leave no man behind" but I sulked in my room watching a Hogan's Heroes marathon instead with Ezell's Elvis guy shouting "Be somebody!" every 20 minutes because apparently fried fish is the key to success and I should've eaten more of it. I proposed to Lori about once a week after that but she didn't say yes until I got home and took a knee and did it for real. We have two sons, the same age as Alexander and Tanner.

"Tanner and Alexander were BFFs (Best Friends Forever)," Zuvers said. "They were peas in a pod."

They spent their summer days in the backyard playing with Tonka trucks. They had a front loader and dump trucks and sometimes they would scoop dirt out of the garden. "I didn't like that, but all it ever took was a stern look," she said.

Alexander was in the third grade and just starting to read chapter books. "He was devastated whenever he got a red mark on his homework," Zuvers said. "He got a purple mark one day, which means excellent. He was so proud we had to call his sisters and grandparents."

He was also the family handyman. "If he had tools and could tear something apart he would but usually couldn't get it back together again," Zuvers said. "He was always helping with home improvement projects. The house was in foreclosure when we moved in and lots of work needed to be done. He was right in the thick of it pounding nails, hammer and saw. He loved dry wall mud and sanding and helped with wiring. We built a platform so he could reach the workbench.

"Tanner was my baby and my namesake, the most like me," Zuvers said. "He was a storyteller. He could weave a yarn and suck everybody in but then he was like, "Naw, I was just foolin' ya.' How does a four-year-old do that?

"He loved to ride bikes with Alexander," Zuvers said. "When Alexander started jumping ramps he got off training wheels. Training wheels and ramps do not work so good together. His first jump, he was wearing a motorcycle helmet and got a long start in the driveway. He did OK until he got to the curb. He hit the handle bars and the chin strap sliced his chin. He needed a couple stitches."

Alexander had a scar on his forehead. He got that after jumping off their neighbor's porch.

Andrew was a book worm and proud computer geek, "He was content to play games all day," Zuvers said. "He'd get mad as a hornet when I made him go outside. He was a huge Star Wars fan. When the last movie came out it was really hard. We would have been standing in line at midnight to see it."

She still has a tub full of his Star Wars toys. No one has touched them and no one ever will.

Each of the boys was born exactly 1 year, 11 months and 15 days apart. "Nobody planned it that way," Zuvers said. "They were too close together but it was a blessing really. They shared a bedroom and they were interested in the same things. They were together all the time, rarely ever fought. They were loving and polite; pleases and thank you's, always quick to say 'Hey neighbor.'

"Some days I like to surround myself with stuff from when the kids were here," Zuvers said. "Other days I can't stand it at all. We watched 'Home Alone' at least a thousand times."

===

Two grid squares is an easy walk so I started hitting the woods again in September 2017, whenever the weather was nice and the landowners let me. Some are very nice. Others have never returned my messages so I leave them alone and stay off their land.

Allen Cryer owns all of the land on the west side of the St. Joe River and his wife knows one of my cousins. That's not really surprising since my maternal grandfather had 13 brothers and sisters. I'm related to every Cogswell in the phonebook here and their kids have spread out all over the world. I found a second cousin in 1994 as soon as I got off the plane in Seoul, South Korea, and in 2003 I found a first cousin-once-removed in Kuwait City. My mom's family emigrated from Ireland during the Potato Famine in the 1840s and the only place I haven't met a cousin was in Shannon on Saint Patrick's Day 2008. It was a military flight with a two-hour layover and I spent most of my time staring at green liquor bottles in the duty free shop. We couldn't drink or even leave the terminal.

Mrs. Cryer said I could walk the woods any time before deer season and I probably wouldn't get shot so I went out the next day and parked on Oliver's

Bridge. The bridge is a popular place judging by the number of beer cans that crunched under foot. McClanahan said he found quite a few meth labs down there so I stepped carefully. The bottom ground is a natural picnic spot when the mud is dry, with lots of shade and almost no vegetation. The old bridgehead is still there and you can fish off it.

It's impossible to get lost on Cryer's property because you can always hear the Turnpike traffic and the St. Joe is always on your left but it was still weird. My first walk was the exact opposite of lost – I always knew where I was and how to get back but I had no idea where I was going. There were no more patterns to follow. Nobody saw what happened on Nov. 26, 2010, or what happened during the floods in 2011. Anything Skelton left would have been Plinko chips floating between trees. The current carries everything downstream but not in straight lines. The river meanders and branches and loops back on itself. There's an oxbow just south of the campground where the St. Joe even re-connected with itself. Waist-high weeds cover everything close to the river and wrap around trees packed so tight their branches touch. Smaller trees grew out on the prairie but dead grass washes over everything in waves. It's so thick it feels like stepping on a mattress.

I decided to look for shoes because they should be more durable than clothes and easier to spot than skeletal remains. I didn't want to be surprised by bones anyway. I figured if I spotted a shoe I'd move in slower. At the first hint of anything significant I planned to throw a yellow reflective belt at it and call 911. Then I'd step back and wait for somebody to come and see me pointing at it. I don't know if I ever got close to anything. I could have walked right by or stepped over all of it. Another 500 volunteers could wade through it all shoulder-to-shoulder and never see anything on the ground. Even if they cut the weeds and pulled grass and raked through the dirt the odds are just as likely we'd have to do it all over on the other side of the river.

And there is always the chance I'm wrong.

Chapter 15

Relue Returns

Rudy Relue woke up in October 2016 and started tracking his own patterns of information. A year later he sent his findings to The Bryan Times in a memo titled "Murder they wrought" and asked for an independent investigation to expose corruption in the police department.

Relue said a city cop tried to date his daughter Andrea Andrews months before the fatal accident on May 29, 2010, but "her lack of interest in him only fueled his desire for her more" and things got creepy. "She had told me just prior to her death that he was making her very uncomfortable and she felt he was a 'stalker' (dangerous)," he wrote.

That guy and his partner "effectively murdered my daughter," Relue wrote. "The throwing of the spike strips in front of a two-wheel vehicle was intentional homicide."

Those guys stalked Andrea to O'Bryan's Pub that night, Relue wrote. He claimed they staked it out and waited, and when she left on Weisner's bike they followed and pulled them over. Weisner even gave them his license before he panicked, took off and crashed, he wrote.

After I got Relue's letter I dropped Freedom of Information Act requests for Weisner's case files at the Williams County Court of Common Pleas, the Bryan Police Department and the Ohio State Highway Patrol Post that did the accident reconstruction. I don't think the accident happened the way Rudy wants to remember it.

Andrews, an oncology nurse at the Fulton County Health Center in Wauseon, went to O'Bryans with friends at 10 p.m. May 29, 2010. Cory Cassidy, the son of one of her friends, arrived with Adam Weisner at 1 a.m.

Cassidy's statement was that "Andrews was coming on to him because another guy at the bar was hitting on her and she wanted to get away from him," according to the BPD report, filed by Sgt. Jeff Ridgway.

Shannon Keil, a friend in Andrews' group, stated she knew that other guy and he was the friend of a co-worker from the local hospital.

Cassidy said he had a girlfriend so he introduced Andrews to Weisner – there were no hard feelings and she bought both of them a drink, a beer for one and a Captain Morgan with Coke for the other.

Keil said the other guy returned to her table at approximately 1:30 a.m. and Andrews spent the rest her time with Weisner.

Cassidy started feeling like a third wheel so he finished his beer and went outside to give them some space. He said at 2:05 a.m., "right after the bartender told everyone to drink their drinks," they walked out and started kissing, and he heard Weisner say "This is not the place to do that."

Weisner gave Andrews his helmet and they got onto his motorcycle.

Cassidy stated he told them to "Be careful and be aware of the police" because he had seen one patrol car at the Sunoco gas station across the street and half a block west and another in the Rite Aid Pharmacy parking lot, two blocks east.

He said Weisner "went fast" out of the parking lot and the patrol car from the gas station took off after him right away.

===

Three police officers were on duty in Bryan at 2 a.m. May 29, 2010. Patrolman Sam Yoh was staged at the gas station and initiated the pursuit. Patrolman Tony Plotts was staged in the pharmacy parking lot at 1221 W. High St. and Sgt. Jeff Ridgway, the shift leader, was at the police station at 304 W. High St.

At 2:21 a.m., Yoh radioed that he was attempting to stop a motorcycle "and it appears the driver isn't going to," according to the report. He said they were driving south on South Lebanon Street and the motorcycle had just run a stop sign turning east onto Parkview Avenue. Within the same minute he reported the accident in the driveway at 243 S. Portland St.

It's 460 yards from South Lebanon Street to South Portland Street. I can drive it in my 2005 Ford Escape from stop sign to stop sign in 47.04 seconds at 25 miles per hour (five miles over the posted speed limit). Weisner was traveling an estimated 45 miles per hour with a running start. He would have cleared the same distance in 20.9 seconds or less.

Ridgway was 528 yards away in his office. If he had been in his cruiser with the engine running and rolled out as soon as Weisner made the turn on to Parkview and punched it up to 45 miles per hour, he would have arrived four seconds after the crash.

Plotts was in his cruiser with the engine running but he was 1,584 yards away. Under the same conditions his best time could have been 1 minute, 12 seconds.

In fact, Plotts arrived before Ridgway. He was putting handcuffs on Weisner when the sergeant pulled up. Yoh was next to Andrews, checking for a pulse and starting CPR.

Once the ambulances left, Ridgway and Trooper Matt Gardner, of the Ohio State Highway Patrol, surveyed the scene. They found skid marks on the roadway west of the curb on the left side of the driveway. "This skid mark went to the curb and over the top of it," Ridgway's report said. "It could be observed in the grass, tire marks that led to a large shrub/bush on the southwest corner of 243 S. Portland St."

He also found a black helmet with a face shield 30 feet away from where Andrews had lain, with white scuff marks on the right-hand side. "I asked Yoh if the passenger was wearing a helmet and he stated he did see the passenger wearing a black helmet," Ridgway noted in his report.

Cassidy's mother, Charlotte, checked in on Weisner two days after the accident and gave her statement to police the same day. She said Weisner ran from the police because he panicked. When she asked about the accident, he told her he "had no eye protection on and his eyes were tearing up."

Weisner said he never even saw the turn, and there is no record of stop strips being deployed.

Andrea Lynn Relue Andrews was 41 years old with three sons.

Chapter 16

Montana

Andrew, Alexander and Tanner Skelton were 9, 7 and 5 years old when they disappeared Nov. 26, 2010.

On Sept. 20, 2017, a cleaning crew in Missoula, Montana, found a box with human remains in a shed behind the house at 1266 South 12th St. and called police. They had been sent to refurbish the residence after a tenant had been evicted. The box contained teeth, a lower jaw bone, several smaller unspecified bones and some rocks, according to Missoula Police Sgt. Travis Welch.

Montana State Crime Lab forensic analysts and the University of Montana determined the remains were of children and "likely modern and not archaeological," Welch said. Estimated ages of the children were 2-4 years old, 5-8 years old and 6-10 years old when they died. Gender and family relationships have yet to be determined. The time and cause of their deaths also remains unknown. No other evidence was found during the September warrant search. The remains have been sent to the University of North Texas for DNA testing but that process could take months.

Brewer, in Lansing, got notice on Dec. 14, 2017, after Montana police found a possible match to the ages from Morenci through the National Missing and Unidentified Persons System.

"There has been nothing previously reported to

police linking the brothers to Montana, and it is not known at this time if the remains are from related siblings," Brewer said in a press release the next morning. "Further forensic testing has been requested by police in Montana that may provide more answers. Until this testing is completed and additional investigation by law enforcement in Montana occurs, it cannot be determined if these remains belong to the missing Skelton brothers."

Larry Weeks, from his office in Eaton Rapids, urged caution. "Any conversation about connections is highly speculative," he said. "The only connection so far is the ages; no genetics. Everybody needs to take a step back and allow the process to work itself through before we make any assumptions about potential connections.

"We took in a lot of tips and this is just one that's now public," Weeks said. "Like every tip, I think it's important to step back and work logically from an investigative standpoint. If this comes to fruition so be it, but we really don't know anything yet."

Dec. 14 was also the opening night for "Star Wars: The Last Jedi" and Tanya Zuvers should have been bundling up the boys and getting ready to stand in line at the midnight debut. Instead, she was at home posting an official statement on social media to keep reporters away: "This information has just been presented to our family within the last several hours," she wrote. "We are processing it and hopeful that we will have answers soon. We are thankful for all your thoughts and prayers."

My phone rang five days later and it was Greg Hembree, the retired military intelligence analyst.

"Montana?! That's a hell of a ways to go, man," he said. "I've been there, to Missoula and Helena, and nobody just accidentally ends up there. Everybody passes through going somewhere else. If they stop it's for a very deliberate reason because that's a considerable jump north from the Interstates.

"This may seem like a good lead but how many families have three boys that same age range," Hembree said. "It was a leap that they even did a press release. I'm sure Brewer rolled his eyes a little before he said 'Yeah, I'll get right on that.'

"I'm not feeling it and I can't really see Montana happening," Hembree said. "If somebody had the boys and wanted to get them excited about a road trip they could've been like 'Hey, let's go see Mount Rushmore, Devil's Tower and the Crazy Horse monument' but that wouldn't be the place to go. Disney or Six Flags maybe; not Mount Rushmore. I just don't see that at all."

I told him about my last walk through the woods with grass and weeds and floods and that the oxbow on the St. Joe River, where I think any remains are likely to be, is probably a mud hole.

He said "Yeah, Mother Nature's good at that," but the oxbow is exactly where we should go. "People would have seen that as crappy water and they wouldn't want anything to do with it," he said. "Nobody would have accepted liability. Volunteers getting hurt in the search would have been bad press and nobody wanted that.

"Now is actually the best time to go," Hembree said. "The vegetation won't be as robust."

So we did.

Chapter 17

South Woods

When I called Doug Rowland, who owns the Lazy River Campground, and asked for permission to walk his woods, he fired back with a question of his own. "If aliens landed, and if they land I want them to land on my property, how much would media pay for the story?" he asked.

During the 2010 search, Toledo television channels 11 and 13 both interviewed Rowland outside his office while teams walked the campground and everything west of the St. Joseph River. Nancy Grace, over at CNN, picked up the story and gave it national exposure. Three weeks later Rowland was at The Bar (which really is called the The Bar) in Montpelier enjoying his two seconds of fame every time he was recognized.

His point, he said, was that the kids weren't there or anywhere near the campground.

"I tend to believe him (John Skelton)," Rowland said. "Given the circumstances of his life and what all was going on with his wife, ex-wife as a sex offender. And I believe he loved his kids because I saw how he treated them."

Rowland said he remembered the family because they camped at the Lazy River when the kids were young. Tanner was a baby and Andrew and Alexander were toddlers. He said he remembered them because Andrew and Alexander both wore glasses.

"Not too long before (the disappearance), 60 Minutes or 20/20 did a show on underground networks," Rowland said. "I watched it and they showed exactly how they did it. Kids get transferred several times. People receiving them don't know the kids' names and the kids don't know the names of the people. Nobody knows names either way and that makes it all impossible to track. The show was pretty in-depth.

"If you believe his story about giving the kids away, it wouldn't surprise me to know that authorities posted the Montana stuff to push him in prison," Rowland said. "You know, to get him upset and then get him to talk.

"Police did a fabulous job looking around here," Rowland said. "We had snow on the ground but no human tracks. If (Skelton) had been here all they had to do was follow the tracks to find the kids. They came out with buses full of people. It was opening day of gun season and they pushed every deer out of here within two miles. They came with tracking dogs and search and rescue dogs and those dogs for finding dead people. We had ten to 15 feet of ice around the edge of the ponds so he would have had to throw bodies at least that far but they brought out boats and searched the ponds anyway.

"They didn't hold anything back but all that time could have been spent better elsewhere," Rowland said. "The kids would have been five to six feet apart and easy to find, but nobody found anything.

"Still to this day when I'm out hunting or tracking I look for signs," Rowland said. "It's been seven years and I haven't found anything."

I don't doubt Rowland believes what he said but I think there are errors:

In 2010 I covered the campground search. It was cold and there was ice on the ponds but I don't remember any snow. We could both be right, according to National Weather Service Meteorologist Chris Roller. He said there were trace amounts of snow in the area before Dec. 2 and less than half an inch that day.

"It all depends on what time people were out," Roller said. "Snow tends to freeze overnight and melt during the day."

Rolland's snow could have melted off before I arrived.

I don't think there were any cadaver dogs in the woods, like he remembered. The only record of cadaver dogs used during the search was at the Williams County Landfill. I saw one dog in the woods on Dec. 2 and it was wearing an orange search and rescue vest.

The kid's glasses are also an issue – Alexander wore them when he was young but Andrew and Tanner did not. When I had talked to Zuvers, she said the family camped at Loveberry's Funny Farm up by Pioneer and the Harrison Lake State Park in Fulton County but they never stayed at Lazy River.

Rowland also said he saw a private hunting party working the woods behind his campground, on the west side of the river, so Greg and I stayed on the east side and never got back to the oxbow.

Chapter 18
The Empty Woods

I learned how to be a sergeant while I was stationed at Fort Lewis, Washington, in 1996. They had a Primary Leadership Development Course on North Fort, out away from everybody else where a Specialist-Promotable like me could get through all of his stupid mistakes without anybody else knowing about them.

I was the radio operator on our first patrol and we walked into an ambush. I knew it was going to be bad because my buddy Stevens was on the opposing force and I saw him crouching in the woodline. I thought he was just taking a dump at first.

Patrolling was a game that none of us were very good at and I didn't care about winning. I just wanted to take him out for the bragging rights in the barracks later. Running with a 25-pound radio pack isn't easy so I crawled up to a big oak tree with fat green leaves surrounded by blueberry bushes, and ditched my pack. I charged at Stevens until he broke contact and ran. That was pretty awesome until I went back for the radio and realized all the oak trees had fat green leaves and all wild blueberry bushes look like weeds from a distance.

It took us an hour-and-a-half to find the radio and I got cited for "good initiative but poor judgement" in the After Action Review. "That radio was you're biggest gun," the instructor said. "You can't call in artillery without it." You also can't tell your supply sergeant where to drop off hot chow and sleeping bags, which was way more important at the time.

===

The woods in Northwest Ohio on Dec. 23, 2017, weren't at all like Fort Lewis in the spring. The leaves were gone and the weeds were down so we could actually see through the trees. The game trails were obvious, like some stoned hiker tore through the woods with a rotor tiller looking for a contact lense. They made no sense but they were easy to follow and they ran all over the place.

I led Hembree down the east bank of the St. Joe River and found the tree with the forked trunk where we found the baseball in 2013. There's an old fence post wrapped with barbed wire right next to it, so it was easy to find.

We walked around the woods for about two hours talking about dead bodies and murder plots, which made me nervous. Four different people own parcels of land on the east side of the St. Joe. None of them have ever returned a phone call so we didn't exactly have permission to be there. Hembree was dressed like a hunter with a Carhartt jacket and a blaze orange T-shirt and blue jeans but I was still dressed like a reporter. I was wearing the same yellow ski jacket I wear at accident scenes and house fires, and I had my press pass hanging around my neck so I was pretty sure I could talk my way out of trouble if somebody stopped us.

"So once he got here or wherever his Here was, what next?" Hembree asked. "It was cold, the ground was frozen too hard. What next? How does he dispose of three bodies? Wrapping them up in blankets just screams corpses. Screams it. Was he really that messed up?"

All we found was garbage – a trash can lid and a blue plastic Folger's coffee can were the biggest items. No shoes. No clothes or blankets. I would have called Towns if we found a scrap of duct tape but we didn't.

"You think he could have buried them?" Hembree asked. "We need to dig, ya know, as an experiment. One hole four feet long and maybe two-and-a-half feet wide. How deep you think? Another four feet?"

That's the same sort of hole I was looking for when I walked the woods with Towns in 2013 and the same thing we found at Ace Corners in 2010.

"How long would that take out here, through mud and cold and tree roots?" Hembree said. "We've been walking around through briers. We're not cut up and we're not that dirty so we can't really rule out a burial."

"That kind of hole would take a lot longer than 76 minutes and you know that," I said. We both started out as enlisted Soldiers and we've dug plenty of holes in the woods.

My only real foxhole was in Iraq in 2003, the first night Cedar One opened up on Main Supply Route Tampa south of An Nasaria. It grew into a massive fuel farm with towers and gun truck patrols 24/7 but that first night it was just us and a platoon of military police running a traffic control point. We rolled in right before sunset and we were supposed to roll out right after dark but the convoy ahead of us hit a land mine and took a couple casualties. We dug in around our trucks and prepped for an attack. I dug a Ranger grave just big enough to sleep in – six feet long, two feet wide and two feet deep. It took about 20 minutes but the soil was nothing but sand and I was digging for my life. (I got about two hours of sleep that night, not in a row, and I still get excited thinking about it even though we never did get attacked.)

Out in the woods with real dirt, rocks and tree roots to hack through it would take at least a couple hours to get any kind of depth and that would not be a quiet endeavor. Rowland lived in a house trailer on the west side of the river in 2010 and still does. Anybody digging around his campground late at night would have got his attention.

There's also a house on the other side of the woods and you can see it from the highway but nobody lived there in 2010.

"If this house was all Scooby-Doo abandoned back then it wouldn't be hard for a guy like Skelton to assume it always would be," Hembree said. "Anybody ever check out their backyard? The woods across the highway could be just as likely, maybe more so."

People moved into that house in 2012, I said. "It's gotta be clean or they gotta be seriously demented and woods across the highway? That guy's been running maple syrup lines since before ... Shit!"

Right then something white flashed through the woods in front of a truck parked on the old county road. I saw handcuffs in my future, maybe even bib overalls and a shotgun.

Hembree laughed. It was just a cat. That truck was mine. We were coming at it from the opposite direction. "So ... anybody ever check his financials?" he asked.

It was a mercy question. We both know police would have done that within the first week, and if they didn't the FBI would have. Nobody has ever released that kind of information and it was getting dark and I was cold and I didn't want to push my luck any further so I said "No, that I ever heard of."

We spent the rest of the evening at JJ Wynn's, the restaurant in the hotel where Surat Nuenoom died, across the street from where Mary Kosier was abducted, and the prime rib was awesome.

===

John Skelton was born in Florida, in 1972, Hembree said, typing one-handed with a beer in the other (Yuengling sells itself as America's oldest brewery but it didn't come to Ohio until 2011 and it was worth the wait).

Hembree said "Skelton didn't hunt but he did fish. Had a fishing license in Florida for years. This is interesting – an old tax return says he was a medic at Walter Reed ..."

I already knew that but I made some scribbles in my notebook so he knew I was paying attention. I hate cold french fries so I was concerned with stuffing them into my mouth while they were hot.

"He was a Democrat," Hembree said. "Know that?"

I didn't.

"Married his first wife in Anchorage," he said. "Her name was Michelle. She was in the Air Force. Damn divorce bankrupted him. Want the lawyer's name?"

"She doesn't want to be contacted," I said.

Hembree went on. "Cousin named Brent lives in Oregon," he said. "That Dodge Caravan? It was a six-cylinder Extended Sport. He also had a Honda 1500 Gold Wing (motorcycle) with a matching trailer. Before that he had a Suzuki VZ-800. It was burgandy."

"Now you're just showing off," I said.

Hembree said Skelton owned a 1998 Buick Regal before the Caravan. I'm sure he wanted me to know what color that was, but I wasn't giving him the satisfaction. He also said there was no record of Skelton working for a trucking company in West Unity in 2009 but that doesn't mean he didn't.

"It means he was probably a 1099 employee," Hembree said. "Wage only. No benefits or insurance. Limited hours available. Did his own taxes."

A lot of truck drivers are 1099 employees and filing their own taxes is a pretty complicated process which Hembree explained in painful detail, probably because I didn't ask about the Buick Regal, so I interrupted him.

"That dig test, you know there's two halves to it,"

I said. "Skelton was a Soldier and if he followed Troop Leading Procedures (reconnaissance is step 5) he would have found his hide site and prepped it ahead of time. That morning the kids disappeared, all he had to do was carry bodies and cover them. The real question would be whether you can fill in a hole in less than 76 minutes."

Hembree stopped talking about the 1099 tax filing process which was victory enough, but I was pretty sure I stumped him. He drank his beer for a while and started talking about his last trip to Cincinnati.

"My hands were full and this guy held the elevator," he said. "I was like 'Anybody ever tell you you look just like ... No. You are Emilio Estevez!'"

Two hours later he was hanging out at the hotel bar when somebody said "Anybody ever tell you you look just like, no, you are that guy I met in the elevator?!"

"We just hung out like regular people," Hembree said. "Emilio goes there a lot. Makes the drive from California, listens to audiobooks the whole way. Stops wherever he feels like it. He said his dad grew up around there and you know who Dad is, right? Martin. Fucking. Sheen."

Everybody knows Emilio's dad but I didn't know he was from Ohio so I Googled it. According to Wikipedia, Martin Sheen was born in Dayton, an hour north of Cincinnati, and went to a Catholic school. When he was 14, he organized a caddie strike at a country club because the golfers cursed too much in front of the kids.

I really wanted to point that out but then Greg

stopped and just said "I agree. Both digging the hole as well as covering it up should be tested but I'm not sure that he was deliberate enough to pre-dig a hole," Hembree said. "I just don't see that level of planning from this guy. Either way, time for digging a hole, time for placing the bodies, time for filling the hole, they should all be separately timed events."

Google Earth is Greg's favorite toy and the human remains in Missoula, Montana, were still making news so he pulled up 2166 South 12th Street to see what was going on.

"What the hell brings somebody to a residential area like that," he said. "It's a suburb of a suburb surrounded by a suburb."

Most of the houses had gravel driveways with cars parked in the yard. There was a concrete pad where a garage used to be. The oil stains were big enough for satellites to pick up and street view showed the house really needed paint. Most of the houses did.

Leo Russel Kurr owned the house but he lived in Arizona. He rented it to Holly Davis and she paid the utilities. Morgan McGraw, Peta Green and Edward Davids all got mail delivered there. "They don't pay utilities so that means either Davis sub-lets rooms or just lets them live there," Hembree said.

On Nov. 16, 2017, police executed a second search warrant for a municipal code violation. "That would probably be Ed," Hembree said. "He doesn't have a driver's license which would explain why he was living in a camper in somebody's backyard." None of them had any kind of records connecting them to John Skelton.

We devoted our last round to future plans and decided to meet again in the spring. We should go to Boston and find Skelton's first wife. We should dig a hole and fill it in and time the whole thing with a stopwatch. We should bring in a hydrologist, or maybe it was an hydrologist (In hindsight, the proper use of participles wasn't worth the effort we put into it). Either way we needed to find out about flow rates on flood plains and the buoyancy of baseballs. A drone would be awesome. Fly low and slow over the whole area and watch the video afterward in super slow motion.

===

On Jan. 10, 2018, the Associated Press ran a story about the bones in Montana. Missoula County Chief Deputy Coroner Jace Dicken said that tests indicated the bones were "more than 99 years old" and dental records didn't match Andrew, Alexander or Tanner.

Tests done at the University of North Texas Center for Human Identification determined that the remains were those of an American Indian child between 2 and 5, and two others between 5 and 9. Tests indicated the remains had likely been buried and later unearthed.

This plaque at Riverside Park in Morenci helps keep the memory of Andrew, Alexander and Tanner Skelton alive. Photo courtesy of The Bryan Times.

Epilogue

John Skelton has never stood trial. He took a plea bargain on June 28, 2011, and pled no contest to three counts of unlawful imprisonment. In return, prosecutors dropped the three kidnapping charges. That doesn't seem fair but it works for the prosecution. Under Michigan Penal Code, one count of kidnapping carries a maximum life sentence but elements of proof include ransom, hostage-taking, sex crimes and involuntary servitude; none of which police have evidence for. Unlawful imprisonment usually carries a 3- to 7-year sentence but elements of proof include concealing the denial of liberties as well as the location of persons whose liberties have been denied. (Further details regarding this offense are contained in the Michigan Penal Code Act 328 of 1931, Section 750.349b.)

A good lawyer could have swayed a jury against kidnapping by harping on the technicalities and got Skelton off. On the other hand, Michigan doesn't have a death penalty. If Skelton had been convicted of kidnapping and sentenced to life without parole, prosecutors would be hard pressed to justify the expense of a murder trial that wouldn't change his outcome.

The plea bargain for a lesser charge bought time to build a better case on bigger charges and prosecutors got a lot more time than they expected.

When Skelton came back to Lenawee County Circuit Court for sentencing on Sept. 15, 2011, he ran into Judge Margaret Noe, the same judge who gave his wife custody of the boys after his run to Florida. Three to seven years was "grossly inadequate," she said. "You have said you do not want the mother of these children to have memories of her sons. Your actions are wrong. Your actions are criminal and you have failed. Their mother, school children, and the community of Morenci will never lose their memories of these children." She hit Skelton with a 15-year sentence, the maximum she was allowed, and then she told him "Your explanations have been ridiculous, albeit more sad than anything else. You have unilaterally taken it upon yourself to determine their destination. Police and FBI are wrought with your worthless explanations. Just plain lies promoting your deception."

The judge has it exactly backwards. Deception promotes lies but lies don't promote deception.

Webster's dictionary defines deception as "the act of causing someone to accept as true or valid what is false or invalid."

Barton Whaley offers an actual description of the process in his book "Stratagem: Deception and Surprise in War." (He wrote it in 2004 but it's already out of print. I found it on eBay for $120, the most I've paid for any book since college). Whaley says the point of a deception alters an adversary's decision by decreasing uncertainty in one direction or increasing ambiguity in another. Decreased ambiguity makes bad decisions happen faster while increased ambiguity makes good decisions happen slower. When the enemy makes a bad decision fast he marches his troops into your ambush. When he makes a good decision slow you have time to march your troops out of his.

Whaley says deception works best when it runs on truth. It lines up selected facts that tell their own story in the direction you want your adversary to go. When he finds those facts on his own he misleads himself.

It's all about bad movies and big walnuts – if I take a nap in a theater I can slip out and get away with anything. As long as I buy my ticket with a credit card at the counter and the usher remembers waking me up afterward the conclusion has to be that I was in there the whole time. The receipt is real and the usher is honest. If I don't leave any evidence at the crime scene I don't have to do or say anything else. Walnuts, on the other hand, have been increasing ambiguity for thousands of years. Wikipedia says the shell game started in ancient Greece and Drew Carey still plays it on The Price Is Right. Drew runs an honest show but everybody else palms the ball. Shuffling the shells is just a distraction. If the dealer lets you win, it's only enough to keep you playing.

In my opinion, it appears John Skelton ran his deception like a three-act play.

I believe in Act One he was The Good Dad. It was an easy role because everybody already believed he was. All he had to do was act normal and decrease uncertainty long enough to regain his wife's trust after the Florida trip. When she left him alone with the kids overnight they disappeared before anybody knew they were gone. My opinion is he palmed them just like a ball and he's been shuffling empty shells ever since, from the dumpster in Holiday City to the vacant school house in Kunkle to the Amish family. As of this writing, that family has been in Michigan, Ohio, Indiana, Pennsylvania and even New York City.

In Act Two I believe he played The Innocent Dad and failed because he didn't have a fact to back it up. He guaranteed the kids were safe, in my opinion, and if they weren't the disappearance certainly wasn't his fault, but as soon as police found out Joanne Taylor wasn't real he got arrested and they issued an Amber Alert.

I believe that in Act Three he played The Distraught Dad. In my opinion he couldn't conceal his broken ankle but he did well covering up how it happened because he kept his story simple with a fact to back it up. His effort to increase ambiguity and delay any good decisions to find the kids has succeeded and every day is another victory.

Also, I believe the evidence indicates Skelton hurt himself hiding the kids' bodies and investigators failed to recognize that because of their own methodology. "A criminalist tends to be concerned about finding evidence," like Hembree said. If Skelton said he broke his ankle falling to the concrete basement floor, and his ankle is broken and his basement has a concrete floor, their conclusion has to be that is how it happened. Nobody in a courtroom can prove otherwise and they won't even try. Guys like Charles Felix, the ER doctor, and John Moats, the retired coroner, were more than happy to talk about the indications of injuries because it was just an academic discussion and they'll never have to swear to any of it. When I asked for peer reviews on their opinions from doctors who do testify in court, I got negative responses. National Association of Medical Examiners President Dr. Brian Peterson shot back with "What you are actually asking for is speculation, and whether in the autopsy room or court, that is just not done." Williams County Coroner Dr. Kevin Park, who I talk to a couple times a year for news stories as well as medical reasons (The last time I got the flu I told my wife "I'm so sick I called the coroner." She thought I was being a touch overly dramatic) simply ignores all my questions. In his defense, if anybody ever finds anything in Williams County, he'd be one of the first people on the scene. If he renders any kind of opinion before that happens a good defense attorney would use it against him in court, as he should.

Exactly how Skelton broke his ankle is the last piece of the puzzle. We know he stopped for 76 minutes at a remote location close to his known routes. We know that place is within range of the Holiday City cell phone tower. We know that would allow him time to hide three bodies. If we also know that if he hurt himself in such a process that could lead to the uneven terrain around the abandoned stretch of Williams County Road O.30, and I believe nowhere else. That place flooded several times before it was searched in September

2013. If any evidence remains, it's either covered in debris or scattered downstream somewhere north of Montpelier. The river runs through town. Nothing has ever washed up and no one has searched its banks south of the Ohio Turnpike.

===

Larry Weeks stopped investigating the case in 2013 when he moved north to the Eaton Rapids Police Department but he hasn't forgotten what happened.

"I wouldn't call myself an active part of the investigation now," Weeks said in a phone interview in September 2017. "I don't know how many tips have come in and I haven't asked. I'm more of a resource now. Brewer's office is only a ten minute drive so it's convenient. We interact whenever he has questions or wants to bounce ideas. It's not on a routine basis or anything but it's pretty common. There are reams of documents and I know all the players. A quick phone call to get pointed in the right direction is easier than hours of research."

Weeks still has two posters of the kids on his wall; one has their latest age progression photos from 2016 but the other, the very first one he pushed out during the Amber Alert in 2010, matters more because it also has a photo of John Skelton's minivan – the dark blue 2000 Dodge Caravan with the missing gas cap.

"The story comes out annually and the media always focuses on the age progression photos,"

Weeks said. "That's the one variable that concerns me. I've stated publicly that my belief is John Skelton did something nefarious with his kids and I'd prefer the media talk about that window of time, when he was out driving around. That data hasn't changed. We've driven that route and we're confident his phone traveled straight from home to Holiday City. It's the next hour and 16 minutes we want to know about. Information about the van, where he stopped and what he did, it's still critical. That's what we really want to know about."

Larry Weeks believes John Skelton killed his sons.

If that is the case, John Skelton knows where he hid the bodies.

Nobody knows what happened after that.

Andrew, Alexander and Tanner may still be out there somewhere close and whoever owns the piece of ground where they may have come to rest has no idea who's there. "It's certainly possible," Weeks said. "Certainly not beyond any scope of imagination. At this stage, after seven years, there wouldn't be much left. Bones, odd material or anything that resembles a makeshift grave. Anything like that ought to be reported."

About the Author

Lynn Thompson is a lifelong resident of Williams County, Ohio, where he lives with his wife, Lori, and their sons.

A 1987 graduate of West Unity's Hilltop High school, Lynn earned a bachelor of arts degree in English literature from Huntington College in 1991.

Lynn Thompson

He joined The Bryan Times in 2009, where his focus continues to be local crime and veteran affairs. In 2012 the Ohio Associated Press Media Editors ranked him among the best two news writers in the state.

Lynn is a veteran himself, having served two tours in Iraq. His awards include the Bronze Star Medal and Combat Infantry Badge. He continues to serve with the Indiana National Guard as a Division staff Major.

This is his first book.

Sources

Group, S. B. (2010, November 29). Mom of missing Mich. boys on sex-offender list. Retrieved November 29, 2010, from http://nbc24.com/news/local/mom-of-missing-mich-boys-on-sex-offender-list.

Morgan, S. (2014, February 19). Hear Me Now? Retrieved November 7, 2015, from https://www.theatlantic.com/magazine/archive/2011/05/hear-me-now/308449/.

Resnick, P. J. (1969). Child Murder by Parents: A Psychiatric Review of Filicide. American Journal of Psychiatry, 126(3), 325-334. doi:10.1176/ajp.126.3.325.

Crime Watch Daily: Where Could the Three Skelton Brothers Be? - Pt. 2. (2015, October 09). Retrieved November 24, 2017, from https://www.youtube.com/watch?v=pBt_Hqeet3s.

WXYZ-TV, Channel 7, Detroit. (2011, May 06). Excluive Interview with John Skelton. Retrieved July 20, 2013 from https://www.youtube.com/watch?v=esbOMxRrRUw.

Rebmann, A. J., David, E., Sorg, M. H., & Koenig, M. (2000). Cadaver dog handbook forensic training and tactics for the recovery of human remains.

Boca Raton, FL: CRC Press.

Missing boy's sister says dad is not getting a fair shake. Detroit Free Press (2010, January 20). Retrieved April 5, 2015, from http://www.freep.com/article/20101201/NEWS06/12 010435/1008/news06/Missing-boys-Sister-says-dad-is-not-getting-a-fair-shake.

Parents say missing Morenci boys are alive by Lisa Rantala. (2010, December 9). Toledo, Ohio: WTOL. http://www.wtol.com/story/13640541/skeltons-parents-say-missing-morenci-boys-are-alive.

Reiter, M. (n.d.). John Skelton sentenced. Retrieved February 19, 2018, from http://www.vidinfo.org/video/15271289/john-skelton-sentenced

(http://www.toledoblade.com/Courts/2011/09/15/Skel ton-sentenced-to-up-to-15-years-in-prison-for-fail ure-to-return-boys-to-mother.html)

(Deception. (n.d.). Retrieved March 10, 2018, from https://www.merriam-webster.com/dictionary/deception)

Index

Made in the USA
Columbia, SC
08 April 2019